INDOOR GARDENING
~MADE EASY

JOAN MONEY

LITTLE HILLS PRESS

Contents

Photography — Judith Long and Alan Gillard
Illustrations — Rosanne Hyndman
Design   — Nick Charalambous
© Little Hills Press, 1986
Reprinted 1988

ISBN 0 949773 40 9
Published by Little Hills Press, LONDON, SYDNEY

Printed in Singapore

Introduction

"Once we become interested in the progress of the plants in our care, their development becomes part of the rhythm of our own lives and we are refreshed by it"
— Thalasa Cruso

Though there is no such thing as a "house plant", and the term is modern and artificial, there is nothing new about growing plants indoors. This has been going on since Man began growing ornamentals thousands of years ago.

New is the fact that today everybody can have indoor plants. Until 150 years ago they were the privilege of wealth and rank. In Victorian times, those without heated conservatories used stalwarts like palms and aspidistras, able to withstand spasmodic heating in airless, poorly-lit rooms. Now, our houses are lighter, airier, warmer, cleaner, and from nurseries we can buy with confidence plants from anywhere in the world.

Selecting Plants

The house plant industry is now big business, and new propagating techniques produce plants at relatively modest prices.

In this book we hope to broaden the horizon of gardeners new to this hobby so that they may expect the maximum pleasure from their plants for the longest time.

To start growing a plant in a container indoors is providing the ultimate artificial environment. Within a house, the air is drier than outdoors, light is less intense, there is less air movement, and no natural moisture to collect. For its wellbeing, a plant depends entirely on its handler.

The principles governing the successful growing of house plants are not difficult to understand. Difficulties come when putting the principles into practice.

Plants need warmth, light and moisture in balance. Maintaining this balance requires patience, observation and regular attention.

Before selecting a plant for indoors —
- Know the time you have to spare for plant care. This dictates the manageable number.
- Know where plants are to go. Plants for a warm, sunny lounge will differ markedly from those for a cool, shady dining room.
- Accept that most flowering plants are temporary house guests only, requiring a position outdoors for new growth and bud initiation.
- Remember that in the early stages of this hobby, it is wise to select strong growing, hardy plants able to survive the poor judgment of a novice.

A well-grown specimen of the simplest plant is better decoration value than a more elegant plant in poor health.

Remember that every plant has individual characteristics; some will complement a room's style better than others. Select plants with the careful consideration given to any other form of decoration — for size, shape, colour, texture. Make use of the contrast of smooth, rough, dull, shiny leaf textures as well as their soft, round, spiky, feathery, stiff shapes.

When buying several plants to be grouped together, make sure they are compatible. For instance, variegated foliage needs more light than all green.

Select indoor container plants for special locations — for instance ferns are not suitable for hot, sunny rooms.

Containers

Most of our plants can be grown in anything that will hold the growing medium and drain well. For use inside, these functional containers must be in or on something that is waterproof, to avoid leakage on to carpets and furnishings. Ornamental containers for this purpose can be of ceramic, brass, copper, pottery, wood or cane of suitable size. Collecting a range of ornamental containers is one of the side pleasures of this hobby.

To estimate the size required, measure the height and width at the outside rim of the functional pot, and allow 25mm to 50mm extra each way to allow the potted plant to slide in and out easily.

Troughs, shallow baskets and trays can be used when lined with plastic sheeting. Disguise this with bark or sphagnum moss.

When an ornamental container is too deep, raise the potted plant on bricks or on another pot set upside down. When the base of a container is uneven, use crumpled paper to keep the potted plant from tilting.

When gathering a selection of ornamental containers to camouflage the utility ones aim for a variety in shapes, sizes and textures.

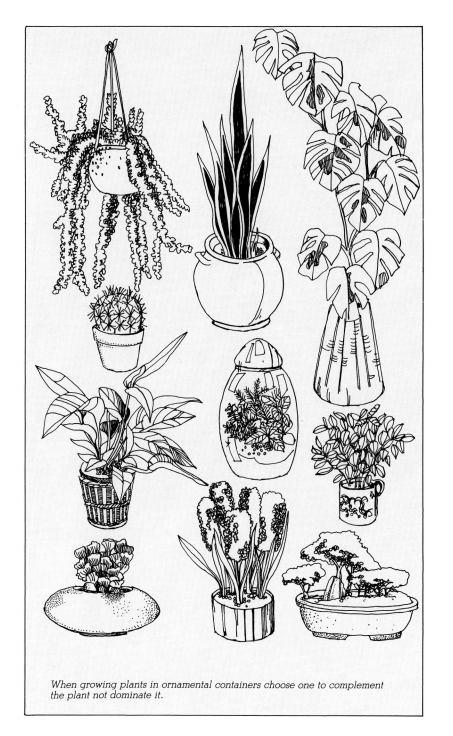

When growing plants in ornamental containers choose one to complement the plant not dominate it.

Display

Success in displaying plants, the number of plants used and their size depends on space available and the effect wanted.

Know the difference between good ventilation and draughts. House plants do not tolerate draughts.

It is easiest to keep single plants in their own pots even when they are to be assembled into planters, troughs and trays. Single pots can be removed and repositioned without disrupting the whole arrangement. This allows plants to be rested out of sight when dormant or past peak condition.

A permanent collection of evergreens can be highlighted with seasonal accent plants.

The very nature of some plants dictates that they stand in isolation. Palms and ferns are in this category.

Plant stands and pedestals are available in a range of materials, designs and heights. They are an ideal way to display plants that deserve to be the centre of attention.

The ultimate in plant display is a conservatory or garden room attached to the house. For those with little room and/or time, the answer is a bottle garden or terrarium.

Garden windows can be used for displaying plants as well as propagating them.

Grooming — indoor plant foliage must be kept free from dust. Wipe leaves with a damp cloth.

Fast growers like Coleus, Impatiens, Fittonia, Maranta should have growing tips pinched back regularly to maintain compact shape.

In planters and troughs plants are left in individual pots for ease of repotting, removal of spent plants or seasonal changes of material.

Flowers are removed from Coleus to keep plant growing on.

Foliage must be kept clean.

Potting Mixes

Whatever the size of the container used, the potting medium remains a critical factor for successful plant growth. Most potting mixes available commercially are mixtures of peat and sand or crushed pumice which have been sterilised before packaging. Base fertiliser is incorporated into the mix.

Many garden references recommend the use of loams with potting mixes. These are useful, but low-clay loams are hard to find in some parts of the country, and sterilising soil can be difficult (the use of non-sterilised material in potting mixes can introduce soil-borne root diseases, an often present danger).

Note: To sterilise soils or potting mixes, gardeners can use Dazomet (brand name Basamid). This will control fungi, weeds, insects and eelworms. The granules are applied by spreading them over a 25cm thick layer of potting mix as a heap is being made up. When the heap is formed, it is covered with polythene and left for three weeks for the Basamid to work. Thorough aeration by turning is necessary to ensure all fumigant has dissipated. (Sowing a few bean or mustard seeds is a test of the readiness of the material).

Commercially packed potting mixes are available to suit a wide range of plant types. Most gardeners find them a convenient and economical method for container planting when relatively small quantities are used.

There is no hard and fast rule for potting mix ratios. They can be varied to suit particular needs.

Some commercial plant propagators use a ratio of one part peat to one part coarse sand or pumice sand, and this is a good standard mix for the do-it-yourself container gardener to begin with. It has the advantage of better wetting qualities when dry, and it is heavier so helps make containers more stable. On the other hand, the water holding capacity is lower and this is why other standard mixes are based on a three parts peat to one part coarse sand or pumice sand.

Fertiliser and lime — for gardeners mixing their own potting mix, the following fertilisers may be used:

- For one-season or short-life plants — to each 50 litres of peat and pumice mix add 75 grams of short term Osmocote fertiliser, 150 grams Dolomite lime, and 75 grams ground limestone.

- For long-life indoor plants — to each 50 litres of peat and pumice mix add 150 grams long term Osmocote, 45 grams short term Osmocote, 150 grams Dolomite lime, and 75 grams ground limestone. (Omit the latter for acid-loving plants).

Careful measurement of fertiliser and lime additions to the mix is essential. Over-generous applications of any one can create problems for the plants. When acid-loving plants such as azaleas and ericas are being grown, a low lime content in the mixture is necessary.

Thorough mixing for even distribution of all ingredients is important. To help achieve this, fertiliser and lime should be added slowly during the mixing.

Sterilised or clean ingredients are easily contaminated by disease organisms if mixed in the presence of dirt or untreated soil. For mixing, it is wise to choose a concrete surface that has been washed down with a disinfectant such as Jeyes Fluid. Once mixed, it should be stored in covered containers.

Peat is a most important ingredient of potting mixes because of its capacity to absorb 20 times or more its own weight in water while allowing excess water to drain away freely.

Peat is available for our use only because it has accumulated in acid, airless environments that have excluded almost all breakdown organisms normally found in soil. With little or no gas exchange, even oxidation of plant remains is virtually at a standstill.

When it is used in a potting mix however, all these conditions are reversed. Lime is added to lower acidity. There is plenty of air, and soil organisms soon appear. The result is a fairly rapid breakdown of the peat in the mix. This is one of the important reasons for regular re-potting.

As the peat breaks down, its mechanical effect of providing air spaces for the roots and its moisture retaining capacity diminish until an adverse effect on root growth and function becomes apparent.

Checking the state of potting mix should be part of routine plant care. It is easy to compare the appearance of the material in use with a sample of fresh unused mix.

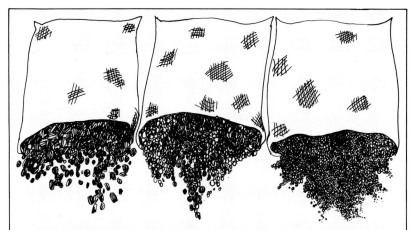

Commercial prepared potting mixes are available for special plant types — orchids, cacti, 'African Violets' etc. — slow release fertilisers have been added to these mixes.

Potting

Always have clean containers. Check that drainage holes are large enough. Have a layer of coarse drainage material such as pieces of pumice or broken pots to keep the drainage holes free. Have potting mix damp but not wet; use a small stick to work mix around the roots, consolidate it by tamping the pot (lifting it a little and dropping it). Do not bury the plant any deeper than it was. Do not fill the pot to the top — allow from 2cm to 7cm, depending on the pot size, between top of mix and rim of pot.

When a plant has become root bound, tease out the roots before re-potting. Remove the old potting mix from the root ball and gently untangle the roots. If left in the entangled state, the roots will continue to grow this way and the plant will lose vigour. Cut off any damaged roots and re-pot into a pot of a suitable size (allow for about 5cm of space between the plant and the pot). Where possible, water a newly potted plant by standing in a container of water up to two thirds its depth until the surface becomes moist.

In removing plants from containers, those small enough to be hand held are inverted into one hand with the plant stem between the fingers, while the rim and sides are tapped to free the root ball. Plants that are tightly wedged will have to be eased out by sliding a knife around the inside of the pot. To take plants from large containers, such as half wine-casks, tip the container on its side, and roll it gently while tapping rim and sides with a wooden mallet. A garden fork pushed into the top of the root ball and used as a lever will help.

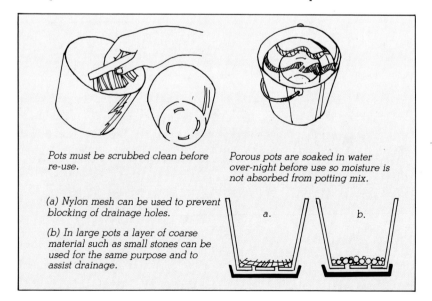

Pots must be scrubbed clean before re-use.

Porous pots are soaked in water over-night before use so moisture is not absorbed from potting mix.

(a) Nylon mesh can be used to prevent blocking of drainage holes.

(b) In large pots a layer of coarse material such as small stones can be used for the same purpose and to assist drainage.

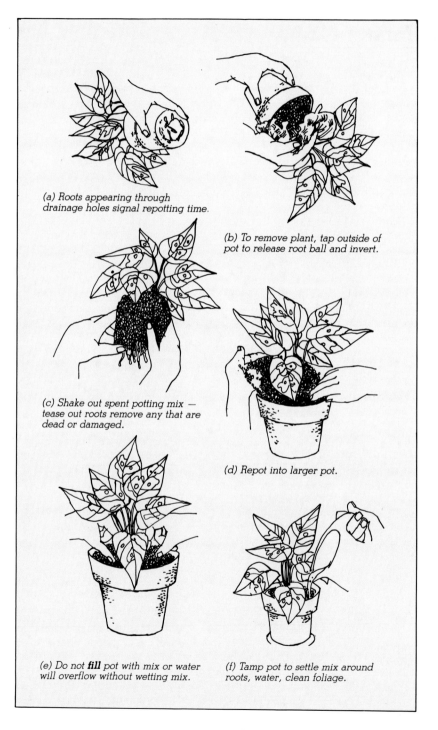

(a) Roots appearing through drainage holes signal repotting time.

(b) To remove plant, tap outside of pot to release root ball and invert.

(c) Shake out spent potting mix — tease out roots remove any that are dead or damaged.

(d) Repot into larger pot.

(e) Do not **fill** pot with mix or water will overflow without wetting mix.

(f) Tamp pot to settle mix around roots, water, clean foliage.

Conditions

Temperature — the amount of warmth a plant needs will depend on its natural habitat and where it has been growing before you decide to bring it inside. If it has been growing outdoors, it will adjust easily; if it comes from a heated glasshouse, it will require a period of acclimatisation. Most plants can adjust to low temperatures as long as water and light are reduced accordingly.

A difference between day and night temperatures is desirable; it is the extremes of temperature fluctuation that do the damage, such as in rooms that are heated during the day but not through the night.

Humidity — some cacti and succulents thrive in a hot, dry atmosphere. Most other plants will drop leaves and buds if the atmosphere is too dry, too long. Most plants will manage with a relative humidity of 50%. Some precautions will be necessary to maintain a balance between temperature and humidity.

Many plants grouped together will help maintain a reasonable humidity; a bowl of water set among the plants is useful — as temperatures rise, moisture is given off and a humid atmosphere is maintained. Solitary pots can stand on pebbles in a tray that has water in it. (Be sure that the water does not come up to the base of the pot.)

Light — all plants require light for the process of photosynthesis. How they manage indoors will depend on the type of plant, natural growing conditions, and available light.

Flowering plants need strong light but not direct sunlight. Plants with variegated leaves need good light. Foliage plants like philodendrons and leafy begonias need less light. Plants that grow naturally in shade are the ones to choose for low light areas.

Water — it is said that plants are not harmed by being given too much water at any one time, but by being watered too often. There is no easy formula for watering plants in pots; it is a matter of observation and experience. Pots that can be lifted easily can be "felt" to be dry — they will be much lighter than when the soil is moist all the way down. When the top of the mix is moist to the touch, water is not required; when in doubt, part the potting mix and check how far down it appears dry. If it is dry at 2cm below the surface, water it, but see that it is a good soaking; then leave it alone until it begins to dry out again.

Do not let a pot dry out completely. If this happens by accident, plunge the pot into a container of water and leave it until air bubbles cease rising to the surface, then stand off the ground and allow it to drain well. Always use water at room temperature — very cold water can be a great shock to a plant. Plants need less water in cold weather and when they are dormant.

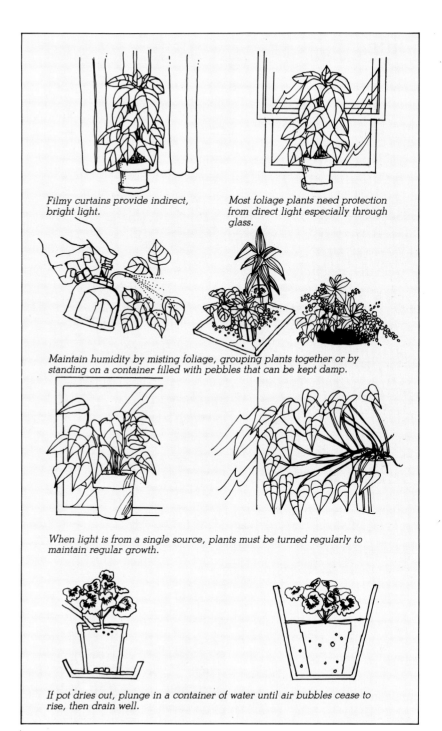

Filmy curtains provide indirect, bright light.

Most foliage plants need protection from direct light especially through glass.

Maintain humidity by misting foliage, grouping plants together or by standing on a container filled with pebbles that can be kept damp.

When light is from a single source, plants must be turned regularly to maintain regular growth.

If pot dries out, plunge in a container of water until air bubbles cease to rise, then drain well.

Hints

1. It is important to make no sudden drastic changes in a plant's way of life. When moved to a new environment, any plant will need time to adjust. For instance, do not take a plant from a low light situation indoors into direct sunlight — the foliage will burn. Make the transition in several stages.

2. When plants are growing, maintain constant moisture levels. Reduce water application during dormancy and in cold weather.

3. Potted plants should be turned regularly, if the light source is directional, to provide even light to all the foliage and to maintain balanced growth, but not if a plant is about to flower: a sudden change of light then may cause the buds to drop.

4. Used pots should be scrubbed clean before re-use. Soak porous pots overnight so they do not absorb moisture from the potting mix.

5. Leave a gap between the top of the potting mix and the top of the pot, otherwise water will overflow, making it difficult to water well.

6. Observe drainage carefully. Slow drainage may indicate potting mix breakdown or blocked holes from root growth. Re-potting will be necessary.

7. Prudent use of fertiliser is necessary to avoid a build-up of soluble salts in the soil. During the growing season, plants should be taken outdoors and drenched to leach accumulated fertiliser salts from the potting mix.

8. While many plants require good airflow around them, most dislike draughts, hot or cold. Avoid putting a plant in a direct line between an open window and door.

9. When should fertiliser be applied to newly potted plants? Slow release fertilisers are normally included in commercial potting mixes. These usually have either short term (up to 3 months) or long term (up to 9 months) nutrient release periods. It is logical to assume that towards the end of these periods it will be necessary to begin to apply liquid feeds or slow release fertilisers if the plant is still in the growth period and it is not to be re-potted.

In the plant lists that follow, the suggestions for fertiliser require_ ments refer to plants at a stage where nutrients must be supplemented.

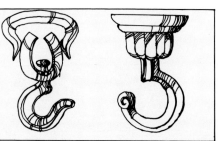

Ceiling hooks which swivel easily let you rotate plants to light for even healthy growth.

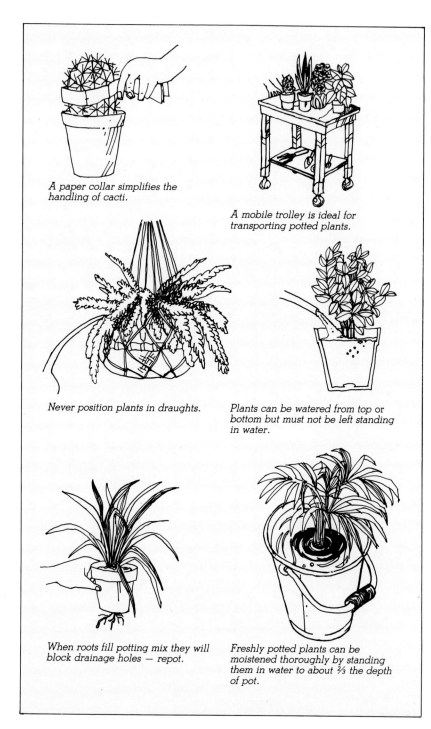

A paper collar simplifies the handling of cacti.

A mobile trolley is ideal for transporting potted plants.

Never position plants in draughts.

Plants can be watered from top or bottom but must not be left standing in water.

When roots fill potting mix they will block drainage holes — repot.

Freshly potted plants can be moistened thoroughly by standing them in water to about ⅔ the depth of pot.

Propagation

Plant propagation is the perpetuation of plants as independent units by means of seeds, bulbs, corms, tubers, layers, cuttings or grafts. Plant propagation eventually becomes the stock in trade of all gardeners. It is the most sensible, thrifty and satisfying way to increase and replenish plant stock. Often it is the only way to acquire a certain plant.

Methods — propagation from seed has little relevance for indoor plants. The number of plants required is usually small, and it is almost always more efficient and easier to propagate vegetatively by cuttings or division.

Vegetative propagation encompasses all the other means of increasing plants: the division of roots, bulbs, corms, rhizomes, tubers, from bulblets, from all kinds of cuttings — root, stem or leaf — and by the various methods of budding, grafting and layering. All these methods will produce plants that are identical to the parent plant from which they came.

Cuttings from leaves, stems or roots is the most favoured method of increasing plant numbers.

Leaf cuttings are an extremely useful way of increasing plant numbers, especially for indoor plants, and for gardeners with little room to spare for a large propagation unit. African violets, begonias, gloxinias and succulents are propagated this way. Use a pot filled with a light potting mix that is easily drained; press the medium down firmly.

African violets are propagated by inserting the leaf stalk into the surface of the medium; the leaf is bent over and held down with a tooth pick. New plants grow at the base of the stalk.

Begonias and other plants that have prominent veins are propagated by having cuts made across the veins protruding at the back of the leaf; the leaf is then laid on the rooting medium with the vein cuts against its surface. It can be pinned down with tooth picks or small weights. Roots and buds will appear at the cut sites.

Almost any portion of a succulent leaf can be pinned to the rooting medium, lying flat or with a cut end inserted into it. Sansevieria leaves can be cut into segments about 7cm long and the segments inserted about a third of their length into the medium. New plants will grow from the base of each segment.

Soft, leafy cuttings lose moisture rapidly; as soon as they are taken, place them in a polythene bag and keep them shaded and cool until they are prepared and inserted.

Stem cuttings are another convenient way to increase plant numbers or to obtain new plants. Cuttings taken during the late autumn and dormant season are called hardwood cuttings, those taken in spring

Increase plants like 'African Violets' from leaf cuttings. New plants develop at base of leaves.

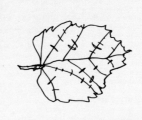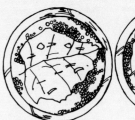

To propagate from leaves with prominate veins cut across leaves at back of leaf, pin down on potting mix.
Roots and buds appear at cut sites.

(a) Plants can be increased from stem cuttings taken at various times through the year.
(b) Remove bottom leaves.
(c) Dip in rooting hormone and set in potting mix.

12

are softwood cuttings, and cuttings from summer or early autumn growth are semi-hardwood cuttings.

The use of rooting hormone on the base of the cutting to promote root growth is a useful and now almost routine aid to gardeners.

Most cuttings do not require a "heel" of parent wood attached and it is sufficient to cut through the shoot just below a node (the point from which a leaf arises and where there is more growth tissue to form healing callus or roots). Plants that are known to be difficult to root can be assisted if the bark on the cuttings is slit at the base to expose more growth tissue.

After treatment with rooting hormone, cuttings can be set out into crushed pumice or sharp sand or a mixture of these with peat.

Hardwood cuttings need to be about 20-25cm long and cut close to a bud, top or bottom. They are set in the propagating pot to about half their length. Set out in autumn or early winter, they should have rooted ready for transplanting by the following spring.

Softwood cuttings taken in spring from new growth are tender, tend to wilt easily and require a permanent cover of glass or plastic. A convenient method of providing this cover where only a few cuttings are being struck, is to place the pot of rooting medium and cuttings inside a large plastic bag with the top tied or clipped, or place a large glass jar over the pot.

Softwood cuttings are normally 10-15cm long, with one or two upper leaves or leaf portions retained and lower leaves removed. Some softwood cuttings, such as Impatiens or Fuchsia, root easily without covers, but these are exceptions.

Semi-hardwood cuttings are taken soon after the active growing season of summer and autumn. They need to be between 20cm and 35cm long and are inserted in the rooting medium to about half their length after being dipped in rooting hormone. Most can be struck without cover in a shady place, but more success is likely when cover is available. As losses are likely to be higher than from hardwood cuttings, a proportionately higher number of cuttings should be set out.

Plant Division — plants that grow from clumps, crowns, corms, bulbs, rhizomes or tubers eventually become crowded and lend themselves to propagation by division. As long as roots and buds are both present on each of the parts removed, they can be established as new plants. Most dividing of this kind is done in autumn or when flowering has finished and the plant is dormant.

The whole plant is removed from the pot and loose soil shaken from the roots. The best new plants are usually obtained from the more vigorous growths on the outside.

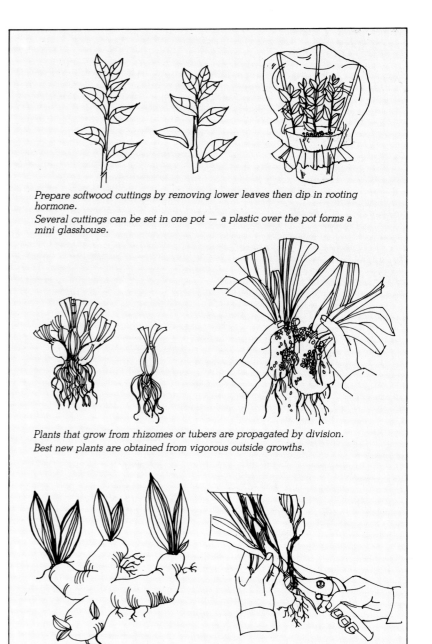

Prepare softwood cuttings by removing lower leaves then dip in rooting hormone.

Several cuttings can be set in one pot — a plastic over the pot forms a mini glasshouse.

Plants that grow from rhizomes or tubers are propagated by division. Best new plants are obtained from vigorous outside growths.

As long as roots and buds are present on each division these will establish as new plants.

Disorders

Indoor plants will be subject to attacks from any of the pests and diseases that abound in the open garden. The most common will be aphids, scale insects, mealy bug, thrips and red spider mite.

Causes of symptoms can be conflicting; for instance a plant can wilt because it is getting too much water or not enough — it is necessary to examine the potting mix to see which it is. Several conditions can have a similar effect on a plant.

Wilting — temperature too high, humidity too low; mix too wet or too dry — if mix is only moist, it could be high in soluble salts, so take outside and drench thoroughly to leach. Plant could need repotting.

Plant collapses — cold or hot draughts; roots damaged from too much water and/or soluble salts.

Slow growth — plant needs re-potting; over-watered; undernourished; temperature too cold.

Buds fail to open or they drop off — insufficient light; over-watering; air too dry; situation changed too suddenly; cold draughts.

Leaves fall — change of environment; under or over-watering; poor light or cold draughts.

Leaf tips or margins turn brown — air too dry; mix too wet or too dry — if moist, drench to leach out soluble salts.

Leaves yellow — temperature too high; air too dry; poor light; mix too wet or too dry.

Leggy growth — light too low; temperature too high for amount of light.

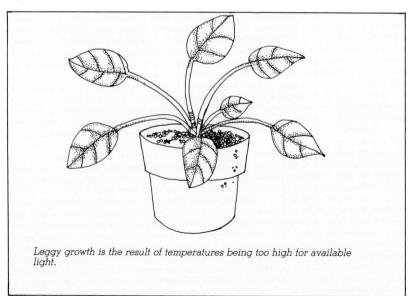

Leggy growth is the result of temperatures being too high for available light.

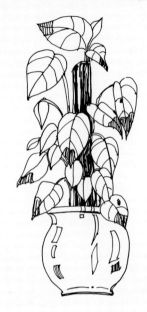

Leaves turn yellow if temperature too high, humidity too low, insufficient light or mix too wet.

Browning of leaf tips indicates mix too dry or too wet, or humidity too low.

Wilting is caused by mix being too wet or too dry or by low humidity.

Total collapse suggests roots damaged from too much water or plant in hot or cold draughts.

Pests and Diseases

A casual glance at the full range of pests and disease problems is awesome. Happily, no gardener plays host to all of them. But most of us are favoured by a few; so observation is critical. Regular inspection of house plants prevents a build up of problems.

Insect pests and plant diseases can be troublesome indoors as well as outside. Where there are only a few plants, these can be treated individually by cleaning the offending insects from the plant with a soft cloth and soapy water. There are aerosol cans of insecticide available. These are useful to treat small numbers of plants indoors.

When a plant collection has grown, it is best to remove it from the house for regular spraying. The advantages in this are —

● The plants can be thoroughly sprayed to the point of run off. (All surfaces are covered and spray material starts to be shed).

● It avoids mess indoors, and a wide section of spray materials can be used without fear of contamination.

● Moving the plants provides an opportunity for overall inspection.

Note: The spraying oil recommended in the table below refers to that used for summer spraying. Dormant winter oils are not suitable.

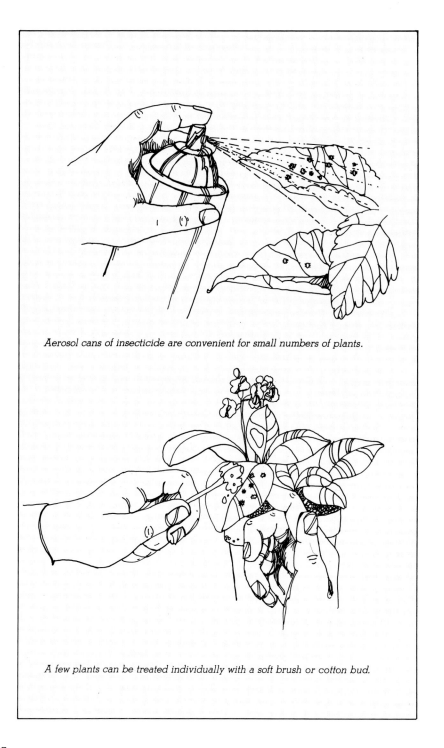

Aerosol cans of insecticide are convenient for small numbers of plants.

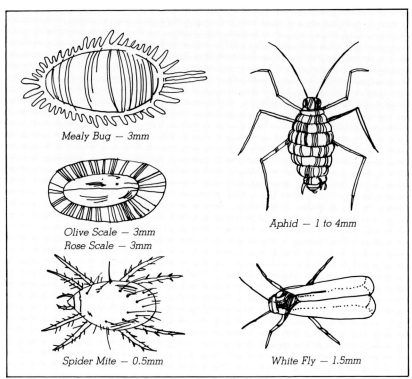

Mealy Bug — 3mm

Olive Scale — 3mm
Rose Scale — 3mm

Aphid — 1 to 4mm

Spider Mite — 0.5mm

White Fly — 1.5mm

A few plants can be treated individually with a soft brush or cotton bud.

Treatment

Symptom	Cause	Control
Distortion of tip growth; puckering, curling of young leaves.	Aphids, usually on growing points and young foliage.	Spray with insecticide. Many are suitable, including Maldison (Malathion), Acephate (Orthene).
Holes chewed in leaves or leaves stripped to mid rib; insect droppings present.	Looper caterpillar.	Spray with Maldison (Malathion), Acephate (Orthene) or Carbaryl.
Leaves folded and stuck with webbing or leaves bound together.	Leaf roller caterpillar.	Spray with Carbaryl.
Tiny, white, slow-moving bug-like insects covered with mealy wax coating.	Mealy bugs.	Spray with Acephate (Orthene) or Maldison (Malathion) or spraying oil.
Small lumps, like insects but no head or legs apparent. Sometimes shield-like, waxy lumps or lumps of waxy cotton fluff.	Scale insects, soft wax scale, various shield scales or cottony cushion scale.	Spray with Maldison (Malathion), and spraying oil combination. May need several applications.
Silvering of leaves with brown or black specks on the underside.	Thrips.	Spray with Maldison (Malathion) or Acephate (Orthene).
Tiny white insects under leaves, fly when disturbed.	White fly.	Spray with Acephate (Orthene) or Target.

Treatment

Symptom	Cause	Control
Tiny white violet or grey insects sometimes seen floating out of potting mix when watered.	Springtails.	No control necessary.
Fine yellow stippling or mottling of leaves, often with dry appearance. Fine webbing sometimes present on back of leaves.	Red mites.	Spray with Maldison (Malathion), and spraying oil or Dicofol (Kelthane).
Plants wilt and often die.	Extremely dry soil or root rots.	Soak dry soil; if root diseased usually no adequate control.
Leaves with soft rotting and developing brown or grey moulds.	Botrytis grey mould.	Spray with Chlorothalonil (Bravo) or Benomyl (Benlate) fungicides. Use these materials alternately if programme is being followed.
White powdery fungus on the surface of the leaves.	Powdery mildew.	Spray with Saprol fungicide.
Sooty mould over leaves and stems.	Mould is growing on sugary exudate from sap sucking insects.	Wash off mould with soapy water and soft cloth. Spray to control insects with Maldison (Malathion) or spraying oil.

Acalypha

Family *Euphorbiaceae*; relatives include "Poinsettia", Codiaeum, Ricinus ("Castor oil Plant"). A genus of 200 species of shrubs distributed through all the warmer regions. Certain species are native to Malaya, New Guinea and the Pacific Islands, where they are used as hedges. *A. hispida* is grown for its drooping tassel-like flowers that can be 45cm long and are like chenille to the touch; hence the common name "Chenille Plant". Others are prized for their very spectacular foliage colours and markings.

Temperature — require very warm growing conditions; will survive 7°C (45°F) in winter, but with some leaf loss.

Humidity — high.

Light — full sun or very bright, indirect light.

Water — evenly moist, but not wet; use plenty of water in hot weather and when growing vigorously.

Fertiliser — liquid fertiliser each week when growing strongly; apply fertiliser again at the end of winter/beginning of spring to stimulate new growth.

Propagation — strike easily from cuttings taken in warm weather.

Hints — need extra warmth to encourage new growth at the end of winter.

Varieties — *A. godseffiana* has toothed leaves, green with a cream edge. Leaves of *A. wilkesiana* have a bronze base splashed with pinks and reds. Many forms of this species have been named. Often seen is "Marginata", leaves olive brown with a scalloped margin of rose.

Aglaonema

Family *Araceae*, a genus of 15 species of evergreen, rhizomatous perennials, all native to the tropics. They produce flowers like small arum lilies, to which they are related, but are grown for splendid, beautifully marked lance-shaped leaves that are about 18cm long and 8cm wide. Markings are in silver or cream on green. Valued for their tolerance of the less than perfect growing conditions indoors.

Temperature — like steady warmth in summer but tolerate a drop in temperature in winter; 13°C (55°F) is considered the lowest they manage while remaining in good condition.

Humidity — prefer high humidity, but do quite well in a drier atmosphere.

Light — a feature of Aglaonema is the ability to grow better in a lower light than many other plants with variegated foliage. Must be sheltered from direct sunlight.

Water — use plenty during warm months; be careful not to over-water in winter. Increase water supply as temperatures begin to rise.

Fertiliser — not heavy feeders; every two or three months during the growing season is sufficient.

Propagation — easily increased from stem cuttings or division.

Hints — very small young plants serve well in a terrarium.

Varieties — *A. commutatum* has silver marked leaves. On *A. pictum* the leaves are spotted with silver. *A. roebelinii* ("Silver Queen") is very heavily marked with silver. There are many hybrids — one, *A. pseudo-bracteata*, has light green leaves splashed with cream.

Anthurium

Family *Araceae*, a genus of 500 species of perennial plants native to tropical America. All have attractive foliage but are grown for the brightly coloured spathes that enclose the cylindrical spadix. These are carried through most of the year and are long lasting on the plant and as cut flowers.

Temperature — are best with steady, even warmth throughout the year; will accept a minimum of 15°C (59°F).

Humidity — must be high in warm weather.

Light — bright, indirect sunlight.

Water — an even moisture at all times.

Fertiliser — approaching and through flowering.

Propagation — can be increased by division in winter.

Hints — the steady warmth critical for these plants can be maintained in an enclosed sun porch when a glasshouse is not available.

Varieties — two species and their many hybrids are available. *A. andreanum* from Colombia is considered the most hardy. It has orange/red heart-shaped spathe, and is a parent of many hybrids with a wide colour range. Spathe has the appearance of being lacquered. *A.scherzerianum* has a smaller spathe, brilliantly scarlet with a spadix that is spirally twisted. It is native to Costa Rica.

Aphelandra

Family *Acanthaceae*, a genus of 60 species of shrubby evergreen perennials native to tropical and sub-tropical America. Common name is "Zebra Plant", and it is grown as much for its foliage as its flowers. Leaves are shiny, dark green with very prominent cream veins. Flowers are in terminal four-sided spikes, and can be yellow, orange or red, produced from red edged yellow bracts.

Temperature — steady warmth; minimum 12°C (53°F).

Humidity — high during warm months; drier atmosphere in winter.

Water — evenly moist; reduce water in winter.

Light — bright, indirect.

Fertiliser — each month during warm weather.

Propagation — cuttings easy to strike if heat is available.

Hints — usually grown in relatively small pots, which encourages flowering. They develop a dense root mass inclined to fill pot, so careful watering is necessary to maintain even moisture. These plants drop leaves very quickly when potting mix is allowed to dry out. Inclined to become leggy after flower or flowered stem dies back; this is their rest period, reduce water but do not allow to become completely dry. Often treated as a short life plant but, given a favourable environment with sufficient heat, new shoots are produced.

Varieties — most often seen are *A. squarrosa* from Brazil and *A. aurantiaca* from Mexico.

Aspidistra

Family *Lilaceae*, a genus of four species of evergreen perennials from Japan, China and the Himalayas. These plants won renown in Victorian times for their ability to thrive in low light conditions indoors with very little care, but they are truly handsome plants. They are used as ground cover plants under trees in mild climates, and the foliage is very popular with flower arrangers. Leaves grow in a stiff arch, are a shiny deep green, and can be 50cm long. A mature plant can be 2 metres high. It has a long life expectancy.

Temperature — not completely hardy, but grow in any temperature above 6°C (43°F).

Humidity — tolerate dry air.

Light — do well in poor light.

Water — allow potting mix to dry out somewhat between waterings, then soak the pot and drain well.

Fertiliser — not necessary.

Propagation — division of crowded plants in spring.

Hints — keep foliage clean; mist occasionally in warm weather. Do not let plants become pot bound; re-pot regularly.

Varieties — *A.elatior* is the one most often seen; it has a variegated form with leaves striped cream or white; needs more light than the species.

Aucuba

Aucuba is the Latinised form of the Japanese name of the genus — family *Cornaceae*, a genus of three species of evergreen shrubs from Japan, China and the Himalayas. Species have tough, dark green, shiny leaves with serrated edges. They are valued in the garden for semi-shaded areas and beneath large trees. A mature shrub will be about 1.5 metres high. They are very adaptable. Such qualities have made aucubas fine indoor plants for cool rooms, entrances or passageways and places that are poorly lit and draughty, where more demanding plants could not perform well.

Temperature — need a cool situation; high temperatures indoors, especially in winter, will cause leaves to drop.

Humidity — tolerate dry atmosphere.

Light — suitable for low light areas.

Water — do not allow potting mix to dry out.

Fertiliser — liquid plant food every two or three months.

Propagation — from cuttings taken in spring.

Hints — both sexes needed for a crop of berries — one male to about five females is the ratio.

Varieties — there are several outstanding cultivars of the all green *A. japonica*. "Crotonoides" is considered the most reliable. Its leaves marked and spotted in deep gold, it is female. The males are usually all green, but there are two male clones with variegated leaves, "Gold Dust" and "Mr Goldstrike". "Picturata" has a broad splash of gold in the leaf centre, while "Sulphur" has long tapering leaves with yellow edges.

Azaleas

Botanically azaleas are of the genus Rhododendron, family *Ericaceae*, but gardeners think of them apart and catalogues list them separately. They can be evergreen or deciduous, but it is the evergreens that are unsurpassed as flowering container plants. They are not permanent indoor plants, but are taken indoors as flowering begins; in the right environment they will last a month or more. As flowering wanes, they are returned to an outdoor growing site.

Temperature — must be cool, leaves and buds will drop if too hot.

Humidity — 50%; leaves and buds will drop if too dry.

Light — bright light; not direct sunlight.

Water — must never dry out; need plenty of water all year round.

Fertiliser — feed regularly after flowering and through the growing season; stop feeding before flowering begins or plants may bolt into new growth.

Propagation — strike easily from semi-hardwood cuttings taken with a heel.

Hints — azaleas are subject to attack from thrips, red spider mite and leaf roller caterpillar (see **Pests and Diseases** Section). Azaleas have a preference for acid growing conditions, and potting mixes are generally slightly acid and likely to increase in acidity through fertiliser additions and leaching. Avoid adding lime.

Varieties — most of the evergreen azaleas come from China and Japan. The modern ones are the result of much selecting and hybridising between species and cultivars. Gumpo, Kurume and Indica are well known strains. They come in all sizes from 30cm to 1.5 metres, flower size varies and can be single, double or "hose-in-hose". Colour range is from white through all pinks, to reds, violet and purple.

Beaucarnea

Family *Lilaceae*, a genus of 24 species native to dry regions of Texas, Mexico and Guatemala. At ground level, a bulbous, greyish wrinkled trunk develops; from it plumes a profusion of rough, long, narrow, drooping leaves. In the wild, these are small trees; in containers they rarely develop beyond 1 metre. These are adaptable plants with a long life expectancy and an on-going growth habit. Evergreen.

Temperature — not hardy; do not like prolonged temperature below 10°C (50°F).

Humidity — like a dry atmosphere.

Light — thrive in bright light.

Water — even moisture in growing season, drier in winter.

Fertiliser — every three or four months.

Propagation — from seed or off-sets.

Hints — an unusual plant best used as a specimen.

Varieties — *B. recurvata* is the one usually available. There is a variety, *B.recurvata rubra*, with leaves that are red at the base.

Begonia

The family *Begoniaceae* has nearly a thousand species in five genera. Nine hundred of them belong to the name genus. They are all succulent herbs or sub-shrubs, with a few climbers, and all are native to all the moist tropical regions except Australia. Probably the most widely grown of all hobby plants, they are prized for flowers and foliage. Usually divided into three groups according to root formation.

1. Begonia x tuberhybrida

The tuberous begonias we know are the result of much hybridising between seven or eight species, with small, single flowers and a limited colour range, which were introduced from South America a little over a century ago. Today, the flower size, form and colour is spectacular. These are among the most admired flowers of summer. Grown from tubers purchased in the dormant state during winter, and started into growth when a temperature of about 15°C (59°F) can be provided.

Temperature — warm, minimum 10°C (50°F).

Humidity — high with good ventilation.

Light — bright, indirect.

Water — need frequent waterings through growth and flowering; allow potting mix to dry out a little between waterings.

Fertiliser — every 10 to 14 days when growing vigorously; frequency of water applications will affect this.

Propagation — from seed sown in autumn, or from cuttings of young shoots removed from tubers as they emerge in spring.

Hints — a position where ventilation (not draughts) is good is the best recipe for success with these plants. Remember, the tuber increases in size annually, and consequently, so does the size of the new season's plant. As flowering wanes, stop fertilising, reduce water, allow foliage to die down. Dormant tubers are stored in a dry, frost-free place until late winter, when they are re-potted to start into fresh growth.

Varieties — B.multiflora is a dwarf compact form with smaller flowers. "Pendula" has a weeping habit suitable for hanging baskets, is usually sold by colour. "Rieger" are hybrids between B.socotrana and tuberous strains, usually bloom in winter; flowers more numerous though single and smaller.

25

2. Fibrous rooted begonias

These include *B. semperflorens*, the "Wax" or bedding begonia, and those we call "Angel Wing" begonia or "Cane-stem". These are the hardiest of the begonias.

Temperature — 15-18°C (59-64°F) at night; no sudden changes.

Humidity — average, with good ventilation.

Light — bright, some direct, especially in winter.

Water — allow to dry out a little between waterings.

Fertiliser — every three weeks during growing season — not during dormancy.

Propagation — stem and leaf cuttings, and by division.

Hints — best when kept slightly pot-bound; keep trimmed or cut back to retain compact growth.

Varieties — *B. semperflorens* and hybrids are small plants, according to type 15-45cm with rounded leaves; flowers can be single or double in shades from white to dark red. "Angel Wing" varieties have wing-shaped leaves, often spotted in silver, and clusters of orange, white, pink or red flowers; can be 1 to 2 metres high. *B. maculata* is the "Trout Begonia", with many lobed leaves marked in silver. *B. haageana* is a tall hairy-leafed plant, with a long flowering season beginning in spring.

3. Rhizomatous begonias

There is great variety in plant form and leaf shape, texture and colour. *B. rex* usually has wing-shaped leaves marked in silver, bronze, pink, red or purple or almost black; probably the most beautiful and variable of all the leaves we use indoors.

Temperature — average to warm; minimum at night, 15-18°C (59-64°F).

Humidity — at least 50%, more if temperatures rise.

Light — outdoors they grow in shade so, indoors, provide diffused light.

Water — even moisture; be careful not to over-water; a little drying out will not hurt.

Fertiliser — apply at half recommended strength when growing, not at all during dormant period.

Propagation — leaf cuttings, rhizomes or division.

Hints — they need good ventilation, but not draughts. Most go into a period of dormancy in winter; do not try to force into growth.

Varieties — there are many miniatures among this group, many are hybrids with wonderful leaf patterns and colours. *B.x "Cleopatra"* is the one with maple-shaped leaves patterned in green and chocolate. The great diversity of begonias is most evident in this group, from *B. foliosa*, with the tiniest leaves and a weeping habit, to *B. luxurians*, the "Palm-leaf Begonia", which is tall, upright, with large leaves cut into as many as 17 leaflets. There is a begonia for every situation.

Brassaia

Family *Araliaceae*, these sub-tropical plants were listed as Schefflera. They are fast-growing, evergreen trees. Indoors they quickly reach a height of 2 metres. Each leaf comprises a long stalk carrying numerous 30cm oval leaflets radiating like the ribs of an umbrella. Flowers appear only on a mature plant in good light. They are red and are carried in long narrow panicles radiating in the manner of the leaf stalks. A long-term plant for a large floor container.

Temperature — average to warm — not hardy.

Humidity — average.

Light — bright light, but not direct sun.

Water — even moisture, but allow for slight drying out between waterings.

Fertiliser — fertilise regularly through growing season.

Propagation — seed or semi-hardwood cuttings.

Hints — leggy stems can be reduced to ground level to improve shape — new shoots soon appear.

Varieties — *B.actinophylla*, common name "Queensland Umbrella Tree".

Bromeliads

The family *Bromeliaceae* has nearly 2000 species of short-stemmed or stemless plants, in 60 genera. They are native to tropical and subtropical regions from the south-eastern United States to South America, the greatest number being found in Brazil. Species are found from sea level to high in the Andes. Some are terrestrial, but most are epiphytic. Most terrestrial bromeliads are protected with thorns or spines along the edges of the leaves. The commercial pineapple, *Ananas comosus*, is probably the best known bromeliad and many of them have a growth habit resembling the pineapple top — a rosette of stiff, leathery, strap-shaped leaves rising from a central crown. The leaves grow sheathed around each other to form the characteristic vase shape that is the collecting point for moisture, nutrients and debris; the roots of most bromeliads merely attach the plant to its host and anchor it there. The leaves can be plain or variegated in many ways — spotted, blotched or striped in colours including purple, brown, white, grey, yellow or red. The epiphytes grow in the forks of trunks and branches where moisture and humus collect.

The flowers can be small, almost hidden within the vase, or carried well above the plant on tall stalks. Flowers grow up through the water in the vase. Flowers and bracts come in an amazing range of unusual colour combinations such as purple and scarlet, black and orange or navy blue, pink and chartreuse. In most cases, once they have flowered, they do not do so again, and eventually that leaf sheath will die, though it remains attractive for some months before it begins to wither. By then it is replaced by new off-sets that in turn will come to flowering or can be detached to grow-on as a new plant. Colourful berries often follow the flowers.

In their natural habitat, these plants usually experience warm, wet summers and cold dry winters. They make excellent indoor plants and they require very little maintenance. They are excellent plants for people who are away often, as they do not require frequent waterings.

Temperature — prefer average to warm, but very adaptable; tolerate a minimum of 7-10°C (45-50°F), though with some species long periods of intense cold can cause leaf distortion. They can take high temperatures as long as humidity is increased.

Humidity — some species suit a dry atmosphere, but most have average needs. The old rule of the higher the temperature, the higher the humidity, applies. They need good ventilation.

Light — bright, indirect. Species with soft green leaves usually need less light than those with stiff leaves; those with spiny leaves take brighter light than those that are unarmed.

Water — nature provided many bromeliads with water-storing rosettes. In cultivation, these must be kept filled with water. Those without this form of water storage absorb moisture through powdery scales, so light misting is required for them. Water can be applied to potting mix, but this must be kept on the dry side. Perfect drainage is necessary.

Feeding — require very little fertiliser; liquid feeds at about one quarter strength recommended can be used several times through summer.

Propagation — from seed or off-sets.

Hints — bromeliads require a porous, quick-draining mix such as is used for cymbidiums; some growers add a percentage of sphagnum moss to a pot full of mix for extra moisture retention. They do not like to be over-potted, so a container should be just large enough to contain the roots comfortably. When grown in pots, they have been found to be inclined to develop a conventional root system and obtain moisture and nutrients in the conventional way. In small pots, they tend to become top heavy; this can be countered by double potting — placing the potted plant in a larger one for balance.

Varieties — genera most often available include:
Aechmea — a genus of 130 species. *A. fasciata,* often the first plant in a collection, has bands of silver on wide green leaves; spiny bracts are pink and the flowers are blue. *A. chantinii* has striped grey leaves, yellow flowers with orange bracts. *A. caudata* has grey leaves striped yellow; flowers are pyramidal and golden. Many cultivars are available.
A. x "Foster's Favourite" — maroon leaves; flower stem hangs down; flowers are coral and bright blue. *A. x "Red beads" x "Royal Wine"* has orange flowers.
Vriesia — a genus of 100 species, has glossy foliage, often spotted and striped. These are grown for their striking flower spike, with bracts arranged in flattened, herringbone style, with small brilliantly contrasting flowers; leaves are blunt ended.
Neoregelia — about 50 species and many varieties; very adaptable. Leaves are in typical rosette form, but flowers bloom deep within the vase. When about to bloom, the centre of the rosette of some species becomes bright red; with others it is the tips of the leaves that colour.
Bilbergia — a genus of 50 species; the easiest of all to grow. Usually grow straight; the inflorescence usually droops. Flowers and bracts are in wonderful combinations of colours.
Tillandsia — the largest genus, with 500 species. *T. usneoides* is "Spanish Moss". *T.cyanea*, "Pink Quill", has paddle shaped flower heads with pink bracts from which emerge blue flowers.
Other genera: *Nidularium, Guzmania, Cryptanthus, Dyckia.*

Bulbs

Most of the bulbs used for pot culture come from three families: *Amaryllidaceae* (Narcissus, Nerine, Vallota, Sternbergia, Hippeastrum), *Liliaceae* (lilies, Hyacinth, Lachenalia, Scilla, Muscari, tulips), *Iridaceae* (Iris, Crocus, Freesia). All are open garden plants but bring immense pleasure when grown in pots indoors, especially when they are brought into flower out of season. They can be grown in potting mix in pots with good drainage, in containers with no drainage (using bulb fibre) or on a base of pebbles and charcoal with water added. With either of the first two methods, the medium must be soaked thoroughly, and the bulbs two-thirds covered with the medium. In the third, bulbs are placed slightly above the water level. Potted bulbs are planted in the open garden after flowering, and fresh bulbs bought for potting the following season.

Temperature — when potted, bulbs are set in a cool, low light, well-ventilated situation until leaf buds are about 2.5cm above soil; then move to a position with a little more light though still cool (if too warm, leaves develop at the expense of roots and flowers). They remain in this location until flower buds are visible; then move to a position in full light with a temperature of 15-20°C (59-68°F). Flowers will last longer when temperature is as close to 15°C (59°F) as possible.

Humidity — 60-70%; dry atmosphere not tolerated.

Light — once leaves and flowers are growing away, full light is required.

Water — mix to be kept moist at all times.

Feeding — with "pebbles and water" method, use diluted plant food when water is being topped-up after leaves are advanced; not with other methods.

Hints — leaves develop at the expense of flowers when potted bulbs are over-fed. When moved into high light area, turn pots regularly to maintain straight growth. Aim at a succession of flowers by planting several pots at fortnightly intervals from bulbs purchased as soon as they appear at plant shops.

Buxus

"Box", family *Buxaceae*, a genus of 30 species of evergreen shrubs and small trees from the Northern Hemisphere. Slow-growing, long-life plants with small dense foliage and inconspicuous white flowers. Traditional garden use is for topiary work, hedges or low edges. Make excellent hardy, easy-care container plants for entrances, or as background plants in indoor plant arrangements.

Temperature — tolerant of extremes.

Humidity — tolerant.

Light — variegated forms do best in bright light.

Water — survive neglect but should not be allowed to dry out entirely.

Fertiliser — every month through growing season.

Propagation — from cuttings.

Hints — can be trimmed. Very hardy, but respond to extra care.

Varieties — *B. sempervirens* is the "Common Box". There are variegated forms which are more attractive for containers: "Argentea" has leaves edged with white; "Marginata" has leaves splashed and margined with gold.

Cactus

The family *Cactaceae* has some 2000 species. Most are native to the Americas. All cacti are succulents but not all succulents are cacti. Succulents have evolved in response to unfavourable environmental changes. They conserve moisture by (1) a thickened epidermis with a reduction in stomata (2) there is usually a total absence of leaves, which have been shed to minimise transpiration (3) spines, hairs, wax or powdery bloom help dissipate excessive sunlight and trap moisture (4) moisture-filled stems are strengthened by ribs and ridges.

All succulents have these features. *Cactaceae* are set apart by having areoles. They are found in no other family. *Cactaceae* can be xerophytic or epiphytic. The size and hardy nature of many cacti makes them ideal indoor plants.

1. Xerophytes — "Desert Cacti"

Temperature — for the majority of these, the natural conditions consist of a cycle of cool to cold, dry winters, warm, wet springs and hot summers; under cultivation the aim is to duplicate these conditions.

Humidity — low to medium, though it is not a real factor; they require good ventilation at all times.

Light — bright in all seasons; full sun at some part of each day during growing and flowering season.

Water — preferably in the morning, water to "run-off point" allow mix to dry out between waterings. Do not put water on the body of the plant. Towards the end of the growing season, water is reduced to allow plants to harden-off for their dry winter rest, when they are watered only enough to prevent shrivelling.

Feeding — use granulated slow release fertiliser with low nitrogen and medium phosphate and potash levels — only in the growing season.

Propagation — seed, off-sets and stem sections.

Hints — potting mix needs to be coarse and free-draining; specially prepared mixes are available. A layer of gravel on surface of mix helps prevent the lower part of the plant being in contact with moist mix. When beginning a collection, go to a specialist nursery; make a start with plants with similar requirements.

Varieties — readily available species include: *Gymnocalycium* — flowers early to late summer. *Echinopsis* — trumpet-shaped flowers. *Echinocereus* — short and cylindrical one of the most popular.

Chamaecereus silvestrii — "Peanut Cactus", free flowering, easy to grow. *Mammillaria* — "Pincushion Cactus", mostly round, *Notocactus* — easy to grow, funnel-shaped flowers rising from the crown in early to mid summer.

2. Epiphytes — "Leafy Cacti"

Not so hard-pressed to retain moisture, these are less fleshy and have a more leaf-like growth. Though spineless, these are true cacti, native to the rain forests of Central and South America. In nature, an epiphyte is variously modified to cling to the host plant to obtain and store moisture, to catch drifting debris and to be in filtered sunlight. They are not in contact with soil, only with humus that clusters at the base of the plants.

Epiphyllum — "Orchid Cactus"

A genus of 16 species. Out of flower, these are ungainly plants with succulent, flattened, leaf-like stems. They are grown for the flowers that rise from the areoles. The gorgeous, waxen blooms can be 20cm across, in iridescent shades of red, rose, pink, orange, as well as white and yellow. A few are perfumed, some are nocturnal. Each flower is short-lived, but the plants produce freely through a long season, spring into summer. Suit conservatories, verandahs or porches.

Temperature — need average warmth to flower but tolerate 7-10°C (45-50°F) in winter.

Humidity — high in late spring/summer; mist foliage in hot weather.

Light — bright, indirect, though some early morning sun is beneficial.

Water — need copious watering through summer; keep drier in winter.

Feeding — plants not newly potted are fed liquid fertiliser every 10 to 14 days through summer.

Propagation — division of mature plants (provide support) — re-potting is done after flowering; from 10cm leaf sections allowed to dry out for a week before inserting into damp sand. Do not over-water cuttings. A new stem is two years old when it flowers; thereafter flowers are produced regularly.

Hints — protect fleshy growth from slugs and snails. Ensure good drainage. Old stems are replaced with fresh stems from the base of the plant.

Varieties — modern plants are hybrids between *E.ackermanii* and related genera. Other epiphytic cacti include *Rhipsalidopsis rosea*, *Schlumbergera* and *Zygocactus* — all are smaller and suitable for any indoor situation.

Caladium

Family *Araceae*, a genus of 16 species of tuberous-rooted perennials, all native to tropical America. Grown for their large (can be over 30cm), heart-shaped, papery-textured, dramatic leaves that come in colour combinations of green, white, pink, red and cream.

Temperature — these warm climate plants perform best with a minimum of 18°C (64°F).

Humidity — high; misting will aid this.

Light — good indirect light.

Water — potting must be uniformly moist, never wet.

Fertiliser — half strength liquid feeds every fortnight through summer.

Propagation — division of tubers.

Hints — use extra crushed pumice or coarse sand in the potting mix to ensure perfect drainage. Keep out of draughts. As foliage colour begins to fade, allow to dry out gradually. They are dormant for about four months. Dust tubers with fungicide and insecticide and store in a dry place between 10-15°C (50°-59°F). Replant into fresh potting mix in spring.

Varieties — most are hybrids of *C. bicolor*. *C. humboldtii* is a miniature species.

Calathea

Family *Marantaceae*, a genus of about 100 species of perennial herbs native to South and Central America and the West Indies. Away from the tropics, these plants are grown in glasshouses or as indoor plants for their foliage. Leaves are usually large, long-stalked, with beautiful colourings and markings.

Temperature — need good warmth in summer; in winter will tolerate 14°C (57°F).

Humidity — high humidity must be maintained, especially in warm weather.

Light — prefer good indirect light; tolerate poor light.

Water — evenly moist.

Fertiliser — every two or three weeks through spring and summer.

Propagation — by division in spring.

Hints — need absolutely perfect drainage; ensure this with extra crushed pumice or coarse sand in potting mix. They exhaust potting mix quickly, so must be re-potted annually — foliage does not develop properly when crowded.

Varieties — *C. makoyana*, "Peacock Plant", is a small species with dark green markings on a silvery green ground; undersides of leaves have same markings but the colour is purple. *C. ornata* has dark green leaves veined in cream plants; is usually about 50cm high. "Roseo-lineata" is one of its hybrids, with glossy olive green leaves marked with parallel lines in pink. *C.zebrina*, "Zebra Plant", has floppy leaves on short stems which are soft green-marked chartreuse above, purple on the undersides.

Campanula (Bell flowers)

Campanulaceae, a large family with many favourite garden plants such as *Lobelia* and *Platycodon*, as well as *Campanula*. This genus has 300 species widely distributed in the Northern Hemisphere, especially in the Mediterranean region. Most species are perennials, though there are a few annuals or biennials. Most are general garden plants grown for their flowers, which are usually bell or star-shaped, in shades of blue, pale lilac or white. Flowers are usually carried in racemes, sometimes spikes or in cluster heads. Most are hardy, but two need protection from cold and are used as indoor flowering plants.

Temperature — need even warmth through bud and flowering stages.

Humidity — average.

Light — bright, indirect.

Water — mix to be kept evenly moist through growing and flowering.

Feeding — each fortnight through growing season.

Propagation — seed, cuttings or division.

Hints — grown for flowers, these are considered short-term plants. Perennial species need a suitable holding area for dormant period. *C. isophylla* looks best in a hanging basket, flowers more profusely in its second year; cut back after flowering and place in a cool frost-free place with good light; water sparingly. Re-pot in spring. Use pots of a generous size.

Varieties — *C. isophylla* is a trailing perennial with blue starry flowers 2.5cm across. There is a white form. *C. pyramidalis* is an upright grower to about 1.5m, with spikes of blue or white bell-shaped flowers. It is biennial.

Capsicum (Pepper)

Solanaceae, the same family as petunias, potatoes, tomatoes and tobacco. There are 30 species in this genus, usually shrubs or sub-shrubs native to tropical America. (The pepper of the spice trade is the fruit of *Piper nigrum* — same family, different genera.) From the genus *Capsicum* come the sweet and hot culinary peppers called sweet peppers and chillies, all deriving from *C. frutescens.* The ornamental chilli is usually considered to be *C. annuum,* though some authorities consider that these two species have merged. The ornamental chilli is an annual valued for highly-coloured, long-lasting fruits, usually in full colour in winter. The fruits develop from whitish, starry, pendant flowers.

Temperature — average room temperature, very adaptable.

Humidity — average.

Light — full sun.

Water — keep moderately moist.

Feeding — half strength every 10 to 14 days.

Propagation — from seed sown in spring or in winter under glass.

Hints — seedlings are pricked out when big enough to handle and hardened off. When transferring to permanent pot, use several plants to each pot for a better display. These can be purchased in an advanced stage of their life cycle. They are temporary plants.

Varieties — being grown from seed indicates that these plants will be variable in the extreme; the species itself is variable. *C. annuum* produces conical fruits which last several weeks, ripening to orange-red. "Fiesta" is about 22cm high with 5cm-long, slender, pointed fruits changing from green to yellow to orange, and finally red.

Ceropegia

Family *Asclepiadaceae*, so its relatives include *Hoya* and *Stephanotis*. This is a genus of succulent, trailing plants native to Africa and India. All have an interesting habit of growth and fascinating flowers. All species are traps for insects, who are attracted by the smell. The tube of the flower is lined with downward pointing hairs; once in, the insects cannot escape until the flower withers, when they are released to carry pollen to other flowers.

Temperature — average to cool.

Humidity — average.

Light — bright, indirect.

Water — on the dry side.

Fertiliser — at half recommended strength every two months.

Propagation — from tubers that develop on trailing stems of mature plants.

Hints — considered one of the easiest of all trailing plants to grow. Must have perfect drainage.

Varieties — *C. woodii* is the "Rosary Vine", has a large root stock from which emanate slender trailing stems with opposite pairs of heart-shaped leaves marbled in dark green and silver. Small flowers are lantern shaped, lilac with black tips.

Chlorophytum

Family *Liliaceae*, a genus of 40 low growing, grassy-leafed evergreen perennials grown for variegated foliage. The genus is distributed widely, in tropical and sub-tropical regions. They are all frost tender. In mild climates they can be used as ground cover in semi-shade, or indoors or out in hanging baskets. They need to be hung high as a mature plant may have a drop of 2 metres. Flowers are white, inconspicuous, on tall stems. They develop a bulky, fleshy tuberous root mass able to store water, which allows them to survive considerable neglect. The common name is "Spider Plant".

Temperature — average, adaptable.

Humidity — average.

Light — diffused light.

Water — can be allowed to dry out, then well soaked.

Fertiliser — not gross feeders; half strength every two months.

Propagation — by division or from the new plantlets that form on the end of the long arching flower stems.

Hints — these plants are very attractive to slugs and snails. They are extremely vigorous growers so need re-potting each year. One of the easiest and most effective of all foliage plants.

Varieties — *C. comosum* has plain green leaves. The variety "Picturatum" has a central yellow stripe; "Vittatum" has leaves striped in white; there is another edged in white.

Cissus

Family, *Vitaceae*, which includes the Grape and Virginia Creeper. This is a genus of 200 species widely distributed through the subtropics. The genus falls naturally into two groups, the succulents and the climbers. From the climbing group come some of the hardiest and most useful indoor trailing plants. Leaves may be simple or compound and are arranged alternately on the stem.

Temperature — average to warm.

Humidity — average.

Light — suffused sunlight; manages low light areas.

Water — keep uniformly moist, never wet.

Feeding — every two or three months.

Propagation — from cuttings under heat.

Hints — these are plants with a long life expectancy. They need perfect drainage and should be re-potted in spring each year.

Varieties — *C. antarctica* has handsome, serrated leaves; will thrive in pot to climb, or hanging basket to cascade. It is native to Australia and the common name is "Kangaroo Vine". *C. discolor* (Rex Begonia Vine), comes from Indonesia and SE Asia and needs more winter warmth and summer humidity than *C. antarctica*. Its leaves are beautifully marked in silver and bronze; the undersides of the leaves and the stems are reddish. *C. rhombifolia* (the Grape Ivy) has become *Rhoicissus rhomboidea*; has glossy, three-part compound leaves on rambling stems; is a strong grower once it starts.

Codiaeum

Often called Croton, which is in fact a different genus of the same family grown for medicinal rather than decorative value. Family *Euphorbiaceae*, a genus of six evergreen shrubs native to tropical Asia and the Pacific Islands. The common name "Joseph's Coat" suggests the variety of colour, which can include green, white, cream, pink, yellow, scarlet, brown and orange, and markings which can be streaks, blotches or spots that can vary from leaf to leaf on the same plant. Leaves can mature to 45cm long and 15cm wide. Flowers are quite beautiful but insignificant and not the reason these plants are grown.

Temperature — look their best in high temperatures, tolerate 16°C (61°F) in winter.

Humidity — high.

Light — very bright direct or indirect sunlight.

Water — copious watering when temperatures are high; allow to dry out a little between waterings in cold weather.

Fertiliser — monthly during growing season.

Propagation — take semi-hardwood cuttings.

Hints — when changing the growing environment of these plants, remember to give them time to acclimatise slowly. Choice of leaf shape and colour is a personal matter, but usually the broader leaves have more vibant colouring. Grow several together to increase humidity, which they must have for prime condition.

Varieties — sold as named varieties of *C. variegatum picton*. A variety, "Fascination", has very narrow leaves. In the tropics, Codiaeum can be about 2 metres; as indoor plants they are usually about 20cm.

Coffea

Coffea ("coffee") is in the same family *Rubiaceae*, as *Gardenia* and *Bouvardia*. This is a genus of 40 species of tropical, evergreen shrubs or small trees native to tropical Asia and Africa. They are fast-growing, with glossy elliptical leaves and dense clusters of white jasmine-scented white flowers carried in the leaf axils. The fruit is a berry, green at first, turning red and finally purple. The plants will flower and fruit in a heated glasshouse but seldom flower as indoor house plants, where the maximum height can be expected to be 1 metre. They make a fine contribution to a collection of plants, complement plants with variegated foliage, and can be expected to live a long time.

Temperature — like a steady temperature 16-18°C (61-64°F); can tolerate 10°C (50°F) for short periods.

Humidity — average.

Light — diffused or bright, indirect.

Water — uniformly moist, never wet.

Fertiliser — once a month.

Propagation — hardwood cuttings.

Hints — do not like to become pot-bound.

Varieties — only about four species grown extensively commercially. The one used as an indoor plant is *C. arabica*, a native of Ethiopia.

Coleus

Family *Labiatae*, a genus of 150 species of annuals and perennials native to several tropical areas around the Indian Ocean. They are grown for their colourful foliage. Leaves are oval, pointed, with serrated, scalloped or fringed margins; there is a wide variety of colour combinations, the secondary colour usually carried in the margins. Flowers insignificant.

Temperature — warm climate plants; leaf colours good as long as temperatures remain above 15°C (59°F).

Humidity — high.

Light — bright, indirect.

Water — keep moist.

Fertiliser — half strength each week.

Propagation — from seed sown September/October in a warm seed frame, or from cuttings of mature plants in autumn.

Hints — pinch out flower buds as they develop. Coleus grow rapidly and may need several re-pottings during season. Not hardy; plants will need protection through winter and should be started into growth again when temperatures begin to rise.

Varieties — *C.blumei* from Indonesia is considered to be the main parent of the modern garden varieties; a perennial, but the many strains are treated as annuals usually.

Columnea

Family *Gesneriaceae*, a genus of 100 species of evergreen shrubs or sub-shrubs, often creeping or climbing, native to tropical America. Plants for hanging baskets, they have small leaves borne in opposite pairs down the slender, trailing stems. The showy tubular flowers come from the axil of the leaves; they are scarlet, orange or yellow.

Temperature — a range between 17-30°C (63-86°F) is considered the ideal, though they can handle short cold periods down to 7°C (45°F) when reasonably dry.

Humidity — high; misting foliage will help.

Light — bright, indirect.

Water — even moisture levels needed. Allow surface of mix to dry out between waterings.

Fertiliser — every month in growing season.

Propagation — stem cuttings or division.

Hints — do not pinch out or prune after flowering in spring and summer, but maintain vigorous growth by attention to feeding and watering. Stop feeding and reduce watering in cold months. Watch for pests; looper caterpillar can be a problem.

Varieties — *C. microphylla* has tiny rounded leaves, orange/red flowers. *C. gloriosa* has hairy leaves and fiery red flowers. There are numerous hybrids.

Ctenanthe

Family *Marantaceae*, a genus of 12 species of perennial herbs from Brazil. Closely related to *Calathea*, it is a larger plant with long-stalked leaves; these are large, usually lance-shaped, differently marked according to species, carried on tall hairy stems. Very adaptable.

Temperature — warm climate plants, but adapt to a winter daytime 10°C (50°F).

Humidity — high; in warm months mist foliage occasionally.

Light — bright diffused light.

Water — even supply.

Fertiliser — half strength every two weeks.

Propagation — division in spring.

Hints — like to be crowded, so frequent re-potting not necessary. Additional crushed pumice or coarse sand added to mix ensures the good drainage required.

Varieties — most often seen is *C. lubbersiana*; has green leaves splashed with yellow markings carried on tall branching stems. *C. oppenheimiana* has leathery mid-green leaves banded in silver. Can reach a height of 1.5 metres. Undersides of leaves are wine coloured, the bands tapering from the mid-rib to the edges. Its variety, "Tricolor", is similar, but leaves are blotched in pink and cream.

Cyclamen

Family *Primulaceae*, a genus of 14 species of herbs native to the Mediterranean region. They have solitary flowers with reflexed petals and stalked leaves, often marbled silver, growing from a round, flat corm whose size increases with age. The modern florists' cyclamen have been developed from *C. persicum* from the eastern Mediterranean and, like the "African Violet", they are now very different from the parent species. The very large flowers can be frilled or ruffled in all shades of pink, red, purple, as well as white. Profuse flowering over a long period in winter and ease of culture have made them one of the most popular of all indoor plants.

Temperature — cool climate plants, at their best around 15°C (59°F).

Humidity — high; do not tolerate dry atmosphere. Mist or sponge leaves to maintain humidity.

Light — bright, indirect. Some early morning sun beneficial.

Water — be careful not to over water; give a deep soaking then allow to dry out somewhat before watering again.

Fertiliser — use half recommended strength every 14 days while flowering.

Propagation — from seed sown between November and January to flower in winter of following year.

Hints — as flowering finishes, stop feeding. Reduce water until leaves die down. Leave pots on sides in a dry shady place. Begin watering late summer and re-pot when leaves appear. Set corm at no more than half its depth in potting mix. Flowering often deteriorates after second year, when corm should be planted in the garden in a shady, humus-enriched position.

Varieties — *C. neopolitanum* (hederifolium) is a miniature species from Greece. Flowers are pink.

Dieffenbachia

Family *Araceae*, a genus of 20 species of handsome, erect, evergreen perennials native to tropical America. Grown for variegated foliage. Leaves are large, up to 30cm, ovate to pointed, and spotted, mottled or margined in cream, white or pale gold. Quite adaptable when sufficient warmth is available.

Temperature — warm, needs 20°C (68°F) to do well, with a minimum winter 15°C (59°F) to retain good looks; can survive lower temperatures for short spells.

Humidity — medium to high.

Light — bright, indirect.

Water — plenty during warm months; be careful not to over-water in cold weather.

Feeding — half recommended strength every two months during growth.

Propagation — stem cuttings; older leggy canes can be cut back and struck.

Hints — remove faded and withered foliage; watch for fungus diseases in cold months. Common name is "Dumb Cane". Sap is toxic; ensure hands are washed after any pruning.

Varieties — many cultivars of species available: *D. amoena* is dark green, with vee-shaped markings in cream or white. *D. picta "Exotica"* is dark green, liberally splashed with cream blotches. *D.picta "Roehrsii"* has pale green leaves, with edges and margins in very dark green. *D.leoniae* is dark green with irregular silver blotches.

Dizygotheca

Family *Araliaceae*, a genus of three or four species of shrubs or small trees native to the Pacific Islands and north Australia. Only one used as an indoor plant: *D. elegantissima* is closely related to Fatsia and is often listed as *Aralia elegantissima*. Common name is "False" or "Threadleaf" Aralia. This is an elegant, graceful foliage plant that grows to about 2 metres indoors. Its attraction is its juvenile foliage — spidery, serrated, palmate leaves that are narrow, leathery, dark green with lighter veins, with the undersides purplish.

Temperature — needs steady warmth, 16-18°C (61-64°F).

Humidity — medium to high.

Light — bright, indirect.

Water — even moisture.

Feeding — every two months in spring and summer.

Propagation — seed (variable) or root cuttings.

Hints — will drop leaves in a dry atmosphere. Slow grower; re-pot only every two or three years.

Varieties — *D.elegantissima* is the only member of the genus used as a container plant indoors. While no other plant has quite the same airy elegancy as this one, a similar effect can be gained with plants from other genera — some of the palms for instance, such as *Rhapis humilis* or *R. excelsa*, or the narrow-leafed species of *Dracaena*; some of the decorative grasses, *Cyperus alternifolius* or *C.diffusus*. *Polyscias fruticosa* has very lacy foliage, and the New Zealand plant *Neopanax laetum* is a fast grower with deep green palmate leaves. Also, there are some Begonia species with deeply cut palmate leaves — *B. caroliniifolia*, for instance, has leaves cut into six or eight ovate segments.

Dracaena

Family *Liliaceae*, a genus of 40 species of tree or shrub-like plants closely related to and often confused with *Cordyline* (Cabbage Tree). They are native to the tropics and highly valued for their profuse, beautifully marked, arching, strap-like foliage that is often carried in whorls. They adapt readily to culture indoors and are long lived.

Temperature — average warmth, 15-18°C (59-64°F).

Humidity — medium.

Light — bright, indirect; never full sun.

Water — keep mix evenly moist; they use plenty of water in summer.

Feeding — half strength liquid feed every two months through the growing season; be careful not to over-feed.

Propagation — stem cuttings.

Hints — though adaptable, will grow taller faster with consistent, warm, humid conditions. In time, specimens will lose lower leaves; though not unsightly, this can be overcome by grouping together plants of differing sizes.

Varieties — *D.deremensis* ("Fountain Plant"), height 2-3 metres, 45cm leaves double-striped in silver. Its cultivar, "Warneckii", is considered suitable for low light situations. *D.fragrans* ("Corn Plant"), height 2 metres, has graceful, curving leaves. There are many striped cultivars, one of which, "Massangeana", has broad leaves that are green and chartreuse. *D.godseffiana* ("Gold Dust Dracaena") is a miniature with a branching habit; leaves heavily peppered with gold spots. *D.marginata,* ("Red Edge Dracaena"), leaves very long and narrow, margined in red. Considered one of the hardiest of all indoor plants. Tolerates low light.

Episcia

Family *Gesneriaceae*, same family as African Violet and Gloxinia. This genus has 30 species of tender, dwarf, trailing perennials native to tropical America and the West Indies. These are long-lasting evergreen plants, always beautiful when the right place can be found for them; they are grown for wonderfully ornamental foliage and small colourful flowers.

Temperature — steady warmth, minimum of 15-16°C (59-61°F).

Humidity — high.

Light — bright, indirect.

Water — evenly moist; drainage must be good; do not splash foliage.

Feeding — monthly.

Propagation — runners, leaf cuttings or division.

Hints — these are tropical jungle plants and require constant warmth and humidity. In cool air with low humidity leaves will drop. Have patience; the plants will grow back as temperatures rise. Use in hanging containers to trail over edges.

Varieties — most plants on sale are cultivars of *E.cupreata*, which has bronze, heavily-felted leaves and scarlet flowers. "Chocolate Soldier" has chocolate leaves with silver stripe at centre and bright red flowers. "Pink Brocade" has pink leaves with silver centres and brilliant orange flowers. "Cameo" has rose-coloured leaves and orange flowers. *E.dianthiflora* has pale green leaves and feathery white flowers.

X Fatshedera (Tree Ivy)

Classified as belonging to the family *Araliaceae*. The x in front of the name indicates that it is not a natural species, but the result of crossing two different plant genera, in this case *Hedera helix* (European Ivy) and *Fatsia japonica* (Japanese Aralia). It has the scrambling habit of the former and the leaf size of the latter. The result is a useful, attractive, evergreen plant of easy culture and many uses indoors. Because it is a climber, it must be staked, but the stems are pliable, so it is easy to train. Leaves are palmate, three to five lobed and shining green. Plant can be 2 to 3 metres high.

Temperature — not hardy, but tolerant of a wide temperature range.

Humidity — medium to high.

Light — filtered sunlight; can tolerate low light areas.

Water — allow mix to dry out slightly between waterings.

Feeding — every three months.

Propagation — tip or stem cuttings taken in spring.

Hints — very young plants need more warmth than a mature plant. Several planted in one pot will add bulk and disguise the leggy habit. Need to be trimmed to maintain shape.

Varieties — x *F. lizei* has plain green glossy leaves; there is a variegated form with white leaf edges. Produces pale green flowers in winter.

Fatsia

Family *Araliaceae*, a genus of two species of evergreen shrubs from Japan and China. Though it is one of the progenitors of *x Fatshedera*, the leaves are much larger and more deeply divided. Flowers produced in autumn are greenish/white, globular in terminal panicles. Valued as indoor plants for their perennial good looks and durability in almost any situation. In frost-free districts they are grown outdoors in shaded or semi-shaded situations so, indoors, they are suitable plants for cool parts of the house.

Temperature — cool, 6-12°C (43-54°F).

Humidity — average.

Light — partial shade, low light areas.

Water — keep potting mix evenly moist but never sodden through summer months; less water in cold weather.

Feeding — once a month in growing season.

Propagation — seed, cuttings or suckers.

Hints — *Fatsia* tends to become leggy unless pruned back each year at the end of winter; needs good drainage.

Varieties — one most often seen is *F. japonica* with all green glossy leaves; there is a form, "Variegata", with white-margined leaves.

Ferns

All foliage is interesting, much is beautiful; but the foliage of ferns has a finely-wrought delicacy that makes them very special and sets them apart from all the other plants listed in this book. They look different because they are, and the difference is that they do not flower, therefore set no seed. These are indeed ancient plants, with a lineage stretching back to the Devonian age, nearly 400 million years ago, when the earth was much wetter than it is now. As the earth became drier, they retreated, but the genera we have now are little changed since those days when they made up much of the earth's vegetation.

In plant evolution they followed the mosses because, unlike them, they possessed organised stems that contained vascular tissue for the distribution of water, mineral salts and the compounds resulting from photosynthesis. But they did not achieve flowering. Ferns are reproduced by the distribution of spores borne on the backs of fertile fronds, and reproduction has two distinct phases. There is an immense difference between a seed and a spore; no matter how tiny a seed is, it is always a whole plant ready, given correct conditions, to grow into a total plant. A spore is only half a plant. In the correct conditions, a spore will germinate and develop into a tiny plant called a "prothallus". In three or four weeks the prothallus sets about doing the job for which it was designed, the production of male and female sex organs (the function of flowers on more advanced plants), one or other on each prothallus — the female containing the egg, of course, and the male, the swimming sperm for fertilisation. High levels of humidity are necessary at this stage, which completes the haploid part of the life cycle.

The diploid phase begins with the fertilisation of the egg. New shoots appear on the prothallus, roots are sent down and the growth of a new adult fern begins in earnest. The prothallus, its task completed, withers away.

There are 10,000 species of ferns known; distribution is wide, though it is most prolific in the tropics and warm temperate regions. A few grow in the coldest regions and they are found from high altitudes down to sea level. Natural habitats range from one of constantly high humidity, moisture and low light such as filmy ferns enjoy, to the habitat of bracken, harsh conditions often in full sun. In between are the many species that are comfortable in the less extreme environment of the "house plant". Most terrestrial ferns flourish in a moist, sheltered, semi-shaded situation, with roots in a deep carpet of leaf mould. Indoors, they can be grown in pots or hanging baskets.

Temperature — average warmth — cold is a major enemy of ferns. They adapt to average household temperatures providing humidity is kept at a satisfactory level.

Humidity — relatively high for most; in the average house special measures need to be taken to maintain humidity — grouping plants, standing them over a tray of water, misting, etc (the latter very necessary in hot weather or when heaters or air conditioners are operating). Ferns need fresh, clean air, but do not tolerate draughts.

Light — indirect at medium intensity — never full sun. Too much shade is indicated by weak growth. If light is from a single source, remember to turn the plant regularly to maintain even growth.

Water — mix must be kept damp but not wet; perfect drainage is essential. Water will be reduced in cool weather, but mix must not dry out. Use an open free-draining potting mix.

Feeding — ferns are not gross feeders. Freshly potted ferns will not need to be fed; on others, use soluble plant foods at half recommended strength once a month during periods of growth.

Propagation — by division of mature plants, from bulbils that form on the mature fronds of some species, from spores which are like dust and are collected by holding a sheet of paper beneath the frond while tapping it to dislodge the spores. The spores are sown on to a sterile medium in an atmosphere of constant warmth and moisture and the life cycle allowed to progress until the young plants are big enough to handle for pricking out.

Hints — when purchasing ferns, gather all relevant cultural requirements from the grower; if the new environment differs markedly, remember to acclimatise the plant in a half-way situation. Keep a mulch of leaf mould over surface of mix — this helps maintain a moist surface and atmosphere as well as supplying nutrients as it rots down.

Varieties — *Adiantum* ("Maidenhair Fern") is probably the best known and most popular fern. There are 200 species ranging from the dainty *A.gracillimum* to the large *A.trapeziforme*.
Nephrolepsis ("Sword Fern") — there are 30 species and many cultivars. The most famous is the "Boston Fern", *N.exaltata "bostoniensis"*. There is a compact form of this. *N.elegantissima* is one of the lacy ones, with much ruffling along the edges of the fronds.
Asplenium ("Spleenwort") — has 600 species. These are favourites as they tolerate harsher conditions than some ferns. *A.bulbiferum* is the "Hen and Chicken fern". *A.nidus* is the "Bird's Nest fern".
Pteris ("Brake Fern") — there are 250 species. These are small ferns identified by their wing-shaped fronds. *P.ensiformis "victoriae"* has silver and green variegated foliage. *P.cretica* has a variegated form. *P.tremula* ("Australian Brake") — a larger species, fronds up to 90cm.
Others: *Polypodium, Blechnum, Pellaea, Doodia, Davallia*.

Ficus (Fig)

Family *Moraceae*, a genus of 600 species of trees and shrubs, including the edible fig and the rubber tree of commerce, from all warm regions. A genus of great variety; several species are among the most useful evergreen plants for leaf interest and tropical effect indoors. The leaf size and shape, as well as colour and texture, are varied but, as indoor plants, their greatest attribute is an ability to tolerate a dry atmosphere.

Temperature — even warmth, with a low of around 13°C (55°F) in winter.

Humidity — do best in average humidity; tolerate lower humidity.

Light — diffused sunlight. All green types tolerate low light. Avoid draughts.

Water — keep moist in warm months, less as weather becomes cooler.

Feeding — every two months.

Propagation — stem or leaf bud cuttings in summer, or aerial layers.

Hints — these are tough plants but not indestructible. They do not like to be over- or under-watered; need perfect drainage. Check that drainage holes in containers are adequate; enlarge where necessary. For good looks, sponge foliage regularly with tepid water.

Varieties — *F.elastica* is the "Indiarubber Tree"; there are several elegant cultivars with variegated leaves that are large (30cm), leathery, with a high gloss. In warm conditions these grow rapidly and need occasional cutting back. *F.pumila* is a climber with small, crinkled leaves; indoors its creeping stems make it useful for hanging baskets. *F.benjamina* ("Weeping Fig") has a slim straight trunk with slender weeping branches; glossy leaves are about 10cm. *F.lyrata* ("Fiddle-leaf Fig") has 30cm lyre-shaped leaves with wavy margins; best when young, becomes unkempt with age.

Fittonia

Family *Acanthaceae*, a genus of three species of evergreen, creeping perennials from Peru. These are tender, tropical foliage plants with beautifully-marked leaves, round or oval, that mature to about 10cm. They are veined or netted in silver, white, rose or red.

Temperature — 18°C (64°F), slightly lower in winter.

Humidity — high.

Light — well diffused sunlight.

Water — an even supply of moisture, only slightly tapering off in cold months.

Feeding — half strength every two or three months.

Propagation — from cuttings of stems.

Hints — these plants object to draughts and direct sunlight. Do not tolerate wet feet; extra-finely crushed pumice or sand in the potting mix will help. Can be pinched back to maintain shape. When growing in pots, use a wide, shallow shape. These are excellent plants for a terrarium or dish garden.

Varieties — it has long been considered that two species were in cultivation: *F.verschaffeltii*, with dark green leaves netted with carmine veins; a more robust and striking variant with red veining is known as var.Pearcei. The second was *F.argyroneura*, with paler green leaves veined in white. Lately the latter has been considered to be a variant of *F.verschaffeltii*. The common names used for these plants are "Mosaic Plant" and "Silver Nerve Plant".

Fuchsia

Family *Onagraceae* — other members are *Clarkia*, *Godetia*, *Oenothera* (Evening Primrose). There are 50 species of *Fuchsia*, mostly shrubs or small trees from Central and South America and New Zealand. All except the New Zealand species are renowned for their pendulous, bell-like flowers, usually in two contrasting colours. The species have great diversity of growth habit from trailers to small trees. They are not conventional house plants but are ideal on open, covered verandahs, porches, conservatories or the new garden rooms.

Temperature — these are cool climate plants but are not hardy; minimum winter temperature 10°C (50°F).

Humidity — high; mist foliage regularly in hot weather; must have good ventilation at all times.

Light — semi-shade, diffused sunlight.

Water — plenty, must never dry out; water at least once a day in hot weather.

Feeding — these plants are gross feeders; they grow rapidly and flower profusely on new growth. Fertilise to maintain good growth, probably every 10 to 14 days in growing season.

Propagation — half-ripe cuttings.

Hints — prune at end of winter, re-pot, pinch back new growth to encourage branching. Fuchsias are subject to attack from thrips, which shows up as silvering on the backs of leaves and as leaf drop.

Varieties — there are now thousands of cultivars, singles and doubles with such variety in colour and form that it is essential to select these plants in flower.

Gardenia

Family *Rubiaceae*, a genus of 60 species of evergreen shrubs native to tropical Asia and tropical and southern Africa. Foliage is handsome, glossy and evergreen, but these plants are valued for their white, single or double, strongly fragrant flowers. They flower through summer and autumn, but a strongly growing plant is rarely without flowers. Grown outdoors in mild climates, they make excellent pot plants when proper conditions can be provided.

Temperature — need ample, even warmth; tolerate some cold, but not hardy.

Humidity — steady, high; mist foliage in hot weather.

Light — bright; sun for half day.

Water — keep evenly moist, but see that drainage is good.

Feeding — monthly. Gardenias are sensitive to iron deficiency, which shows-up as yellowing of leaves (chlorosis). Provided plant has had regular, balanced feeds, iron deficiency is corrected with an application of sulphate of iron, available in trace element packs from plant shops.

Propagation — cuttings.

Hints — good drainage is very important; at the same time they do not like to dry out. Re-pot in spring or autumn.

Varieties — *G.jasminoides* from China and Japan is the species usually on offer; height 1 metre, semi-double flowers about 5cm across. There are several cultivars: "Professor Pucci" is considered to be hardier and more vigorous than the species, with fully double flowers up to 8cm across. "Radicans" is a true dwarf, 30cm, with small foliage and double flowers 2.5cm.

Hoya (Wax Plant)

Family *Asclepiadaceae*, same family as Stephanotis. A genus of 70 species of tender, evergreen, climbers or drooping shrubs native to Malaya; also found in China and India and tropical Australia. They are interesting ornamental plants with fleshy leaves and are grown for their fragrant summer flower clusters that have a thick waxen texture. They have always been a favourite of gardeners but do need careful positioning, taking into account that support of some kind is needed and that the flowers exude a sticky honeydew that is very messy.

Temperature — average to warm; minimum 10°C (50°F).

Humidity — medium to high.

Light — bright, indirect.

Water — moderate supply; allow to dry-out a little between waterings; keep relatively dry through cold months.

Feeding — not heavy feeders; every two to three months; a very light application of superphosphate in spring encourages shy flowerers into bud.

Propagation — layers or cuttings.

Hints — use small containers, as these plants flower best when they have become root-bound; re-pot only when it is absolutely necessary as they resent disturbance and take some time to get back into a flowering routine. Hoya should not be pruned; neither should the flower stalks be removed as the flowers of the next year are formed upon them as well as upon the young wood, when it is growing well. Its worst pest is mealy bug.

Varieties — best known is *H.carnosa*, native to Queensland, Australia; its flowers are pinkish-fawn in pendulous umbels. There are several variegated forms, and one of these has pink young growth. *H.bella*, from India, is a smaller species with white flowers with a rosy centre. Looks best in a hanging basket.

Impatiens (Busy Lizzie)

Family *Balsaminaceae*, a genus of 500 species of tender annuals and perennials from Africa, North America, Asia and New Guinea. Name refers to the elastic valves of the seed pod bringing about a violent discharge of seed when ripe. They are used for summer bedding, container plants and, in frost free gardens, are excellent permanent plants for shaded situations. Virtually indestructible, they are the perfect answer for instant colour indoors or out. Foliage is succulent; flowers are flat, four-petalled, with a long spur in brightly coloured shades of red, orange, pink, cerise, as well as white.

Temperature — cool to average, not hardy.

Humidity — average.

Light — shade or bright, indirect; bedding types stand full sun.

Water — use a lot of water in hot weather; the brighter and warmer the position, the more frequent the watering.

Feeding — every 14 days when growing vigorously.

Propagation — seed, cuttings, division.

Hints — for continued flowering when used indoors, maintain constant moisture and humidity levels. These are vigorous growers and quickly exhaust potting mix; can need re-potting several times through growing season. Keep pinched back for stocky growth.

Varieties — it is now considered that most types are hybrids between three varieties of *I.wallerana*, such as "Sultanii" and "Holstii", with numerous garden hybrids; these provide an amazing range of foliage variation as well as flower colour and size. *I.herzogii* is one of the parents of the New Guinea hybrids, which have bronze foliage and stems and very large flowers. Double-flowered cultivars are available, as well as variegated leaves, or both.

Laurus (Sweet Bay)

Lauraceae is the family which includes Sassafras, Camphor and Cinnamon. Only two species in the genus; both evergreen trees, one from southern Europe, the other from Canary Islands. *L.noblis* is the tree whose foliage in ancient times crowned victors in war and sport, was one of the strewing herbs of Elizabethan times, is one of the traditional herbs in "bouquet garni", and is in almost daily use in modern kitchens. This is a half-hardy plant that does not need the ultimate protection of an indoor situation; but every home should have one and, if there is no garden space, it will make an excellent, easy-care, long-living container plant.

Temperature — average, not completely hardy.

Humidity — average.

Light — very adaptable; avoid direct sunlight in summer.

Water — requires even moisture; water thoroughly in hot weather.

Feeding — two or three times through the growing season.

Propagation — from ripe cuttings.

Hints — can be pruned or trimmed in spring to maintain size and shape. During hot weather, mist foliage or take outdoors and hose down. Use a large container — must have good drainage.

Varieties — *Laurus noblis* is the only one, but it is probably the one plant that nobody can afford to be without — once fresh bay leaves have been used in cooking, the flavour of the dried ones will seem less than right.

Lilium (Lily)

Family *Liliaceae* (related genera suitable for pot culture include Hyacinth, Muscari, Scilla, Lachenalia). In this genus there are 80 species of bulbous plants native to the temperate Northern Hemisphere. They have erect leafy stems; flowers are usually large, showy, often fragrant, in many colours. Being hardy or half-hardy, they are open garden plants, but also respond well to container culture where perfect drainage can be assured — bulb rot from poor drainage is one of their problems. Like other flowering plants such as *Cymbidium*, they are brought indoors to flower, then grown-on outdoors.

Temperature — when brought indoors, lilies can maintain normal growth and flowering at temperatures 15-20°C (59-68°F) — higher than this will shorten flowering time.

Humidity — as relatively short-term indoor plants, lilies will tolerate a wide range of humidity levels, 50-70%; if the room is very dry, try to increase humidity levels (see introduction **Humidity**).

Light — bright, indirect will provide sufficient energy for leaves to remain active; heavily shaded rooms will drain the bulb's resources.

Water — mix should remain moist, not wet; must never dry out.

Feeding — once buds form, apply weak liquid feeds each seven to 10 days.

Propagation — seed, bulb scales, bulblets, bulb off-sets.

Hints — use containers large enough to take two or three bulbs. Use a deep layer of drainage material at the bottom, add extra coarse sand or crushed pumice to the mix. Place thin stakes when planting. Set bulbs on a cushion of sand (planting depth depends on species). Cover bulbs with mix. Set in a shaded place until first shoots appear, then fill container with mix, move to a brighter semi-shaded spot. Take indoors when buds beginning to open. Return outdoors when flowering finished, removing spent flowers but not leaf stalk until it has died down.

Varieties — *L.auratum* ("Golden Rayed Lily" of Japan), midsummer; *L.longiflorum*, late spring; *L.speciosum*, late spring; *L. x aurelian*, summer.

Maranta

Family *Marantaceae*, a genus of 14 species of evergreen perennial plants from tropical America. They are related to but distinct from *Calathea*. Grown for their fine foliage, though one, *M. arundinacea*, is the source of the arrowroot of commerce. Leaves are two-ranked and sheathing, with one side larger than the other. Flowers are small and white, carried in a raceme.

Temperature — need steady year-round warmth, about 18°C (64°F).

Humidity — high.

Light — low light, never direct sunlight.

Water — keep uniformly moist at all times.

Feeding — half strength every two months.

Propagation — division or cuttings.

Hints — do best in shallow containers; low humidity and dry mix soon shows as browning of leaf edges.

Varieties — two species in particular are grown as indoor plants: *M. leuconeura*, known as the "Prayer Plant" from its habit of folding its leaves at night, has light green leaves with purple/brown patches on either side of the central vein. Beautiful variety *M.leuconeura* "*Erythrophylla*" has light and dark green leaves beautifully patterned with glossy red veins. *M. bicolor* has much larger leaves, dark green with blotches of light green between mid-rib and margins, and purple undersides.

Monstera

Family *Araceae*, this is a close relative of *Philodendron*. It is a genus of 20 species of evergreen climbers native to West Indies and Tropical America. *M.deliciosa* ("Fruit Salad Plant", because of the flavour of the fruit, or "Swiss Cheese Plant", because of the perforations on the large leaves). This is a very durable plant, and now it is seen all around the world, indoors and out. It is a strongly-growing vine with woody stems, cord-like aerial roots and large, irregularly perforated, highly glossy, green leaves.

Temperature — thrives in steady warmth, around 18°C (64°F); survives much lower temperatures, a minimum 10°C (50°F).

Humidity — at best in high humidity.

Light — bright, indirect.

Water — keep mix uniformly moist, not wet; drier in cold weather.

Feeding — every two or three months.

Propagation — from pieces of stem cut with three or four nodes — these root readily in sand; or use growing tips with some aerial roots.

Hints — the strong aerial roots will attach themselves to anything. Indoors, this can mean paintwork or wallpaper, therefore stout support is required once the plant begins to grow well. Some aerial roots can be trained back into the container to help support the plant. Leaves will need to be sponged to keep dust-free.

Varieties — *M.deliciosa* is the most favoured species. In some indoor conditions it develops a shrubby growth, but looks its best when allowed freedom to climb. A mature plant produces thick cream spathe from which a spadix rises; this develops into a cone-like edible fruit considered to have a combination of tropical fruit flavours. It ripens progressively from the base; segments are lifted off as they become quite ripe.

Orchids

The family *Orchidaceae*, one of the largest of the flowering families, is a truly magnificent group of plants with more than 18,000 species in about 700 genera. The geographical distribution is vast, from arctic regions to the semi-desert, from sea level to high mountains. These plants are diverse in size, colour, flower and leaf structure, as well as in habitat and manner of growth. They may be epiphytic, terrestrial, saprophytic or autotropic, but they are never parasitic. They are all monocotyledons and are all perennial herbs. To the average gardener the best known genera are *Bletilla, Brassia, Cattleya, Coelogyne, Cymbidium, Dendrobium, Epidendrum, Lycaste, Miltonia, Odontonia, Oncidium, Pleione, Paphiopedilum, Phalaenopsis, Sophronitis* and *Vanda.*

1. Cymbidium

A genus of 50 species, epiphytic and terrestrial, from the Asiatic highlands. Most species and hybrids grow from conical or oval pseudobulbs that are sheathed by the bases of the long, narrow leaves. In temperate climates, these are probably the most widely grown of all orchids. Most modern cymbidiums are complex hybrids derived from about eight species; much breeding and selection has been done to extend colour range, plant size (standards and miniatures) and flowering time (early winter to early summer). Flowers can be small, medium or large, stiffly upright, spreading or softly pendulous. These are excellent house plants for their long flowering season; for the rest of the year, they must be outside in semi shade. They like good ventilation and do not like to be crowded; leave ample space between pots. They are grown in a special coarse, free-draining mix.

Temperature — these are half-hardy, relatively cool climate plants — too much heat and they do not flower; they need a noticeable difference between day and night temperatures. There is room for wide variation, but day temperatures between 15°C (59°F) and 20°C (68°F), with nights around 13°C (55°F), are suggested; this can mean some shading in summer and protection in winter.

Humidity — medium to high, with good air flow.

Light — bright; full morning sun is ideal, with filtered sun for the rest of the day.

Water — when mix is barely moist 2cm down, water thoroughly; it is not the quantity of water applied at any one time that will damage roots, but water applied too frequently.

Feeding — these are gross feeders. During the growing season (post-flowering to autumn), they can be fed liquid fertiliser every second or third watering. Do not use the same fertiliser all the time. Feeding continues through winter at half the strength used in summer.

Propagation — from seed; from defoliated back bulbs (potted-up and set in a warm place, they will produce a new shoot and reach flowering in about three years); by the division of mature plants into clumps of three or four green bulbs.

Hints — the most common complaint against cymbidiums is failure to flower. This can be caused by too frequent re-potting, too little light in the growing season, or from being in a position where they cannot benefit from the drop in night temperature. A flower stem can be left on the plant two to three weeks after the last bud has opened; if left too long, the plant is weakened and there is a risk of fewer flowers next season. Plants can be brought indoors once flower buds have begun to open; moving them inside too early can cause bud drop.

Varieties — a primary hybrid is the result of crossing two species; a complex hybrid has been crossed and crossed again, often more than twice. Some species are *C.lowianum, C.eburneum, C.insigne, C.grandiflorum, C.l'ansonii, C.erythrostylum, C.giganteum, C.tracyanum.* Some primary hybrids used in building up complex hybrids are: Lowio-grandiflorum (from lowianum and grandiflorum), Pauwelsii (from lowianum and insigne), Ceres (from l'ansonii and insigne) and Charm (from Ceres and erythrostylum).

2. Cattleya

A genus of 60 species of epiphytes native to Central and South America and the West Indies. The genus is divided into two groups — the labiate, with clavate pseudobulbs carrying a single leaf and two or three large flowers, and the bifoliate, with cylindrical stem-like pseudobulbs with two leaves usually shorter than those of the previous section, and numbers of smaller brightly coloured flowers. In all, the pseudobulbs rise at intervals from a branching rhizome. Many hybrids have been produced from *Cattleya* species and from crosses with closely-related genera such as *Brassavola, Laelia, Epidendrum* and *Sophronitis.* The multi-generic hybrids have produced flowers of size, sheen, texture and colour range to surpass the species. Many make strong root growth and are vigorous growers, needing fairly large pots. They suit hanging baskets.

Temperature — as with all plants, temperature is related to humidity and light; suggested range is 16-28°C (61-82°F) by day and 12-17°C (54-63°F) by night.

Humidity — about 50%, more if temperature is extremely high.

Light — bright, indirect.

Water — in active growth (summer), these need abundant water; in cool weather and during rest period (winter), water is reduced to the minimum.

Feeding — not gross feeders, use diluted liquid fertiliser every two weeks during growing season.

Propagation — seed; division (leave at least two mature bulbs with the new plant).

Hints — perfect drainage is essential; potting mix must be open and free-draining. In autumn provide extra ventilation to mature new growth. Foliar feeding not recommended for cattleyas.

Varieties — It is possible to select cattleyas, species and/or hybrids, to suit the environment available; this should be discussed at the point of purchase. *C.bowringiana, C.intermedia, C.amethystoglossa* are considered sturdy plants on which to gain experience.

3. *Paphiopedilum* — "Slipper Orchid"

The most easily recognised orchid, with distinctive pouch and waxen petals, this is a genus of 50 terrestrial species from tropical Asia. There are two groups, those with mottled leaves requiring constant warmth, and those with plain leaves requiring moderate temperatures. The latter make excellent house plants. This genus does not have pseudobulbs. Most flower in winter.

Temperature — cool to average, minimum 7-13°C (45-55°F).

Humidity — 50%.

Water — even moisture at all times; more water required in summer.

Feeding — monthly, unless freshly re-potted — not gross feeders.

Propagation — division of congested plants in spring.

Varieties — species such as *P.insigne,* or *P.hirsutissimum,* or hybrids of these.

Palms

The family *Palmaceae* is a large group of flowering plants that evolved about 100 million years ago under tropical conditions. Their distribution was wide but, as with other vegetation, cooling temperatures forced their retreat and caused losses. Even now they are not completely known or understood, though it is considered that there could be over 3000 species in more than 200 genera native to the tropics, sub-tropics and warm temperate regions. They are among the most easily recognised of all plants. In tropical countries, they provide much of man's needs, as ornamentals they have unchallenged elegance and grace.

Generally they are considered to be slow growing plants, which increases the purchase price from nurseries. Because of this and the fact that they are different in many ways from other plants, it is logical to try to understand something of their anatomy and growth habit in order to maintain good plant health. Besides being slow growers, they make good container plants because they have a long life expectancy, a compact root system that takes kindly to being contained in a pot, their splendid foliage has no "off" season, they adapt to a range of indoor environments, have few enemies, and are easily raised from seed.

Palms are monocotyledons (having a single seed leaf) like grass, bamboo, flax, etc. This sets them apart from most other ornamental trees and shrubs, which are dicotyledons (two seed leaves); it also means the leaves have parallel veins running from stalk to leaf edge, no branching veins spreading sideways.

Stem — some are bushy, a few are climbers, but mostly they are trees with a cylindrical, unbranching trunk that can be smooth, armed with spines, or covered with sheaths of old leaves. But there is no central cylinder of solid wood; instead there are bundles of vascular tissue surrounded by strengthening fibres running up and down the trunk, giving palms their amazing strength and flexibility. No cambium layer to effect secondary growth, no annual growth rings; with few exceptions palm trunks are the same diameter from base to top.

Palms have one apical growing bud in the crown to produce all the stem tissues and responsible for the height and girth of the plant. If the apical bud is damaged or removed, the palm, if it has only one stem, will die. This problem is compounded by the fact that the bud or "heart" of many species is a delicacy relished by many animals, including man. This has resulted in species being wiped out in some areas.

Though most palms are single stemmed, some do produce off-sets from the base that develop into new stems.

Roots — there are no woody roots at the base of palms. Instead, there is a fibrous root system developing from a confined area at the base of the stem; roots are all similar in size and immensely strong; as they die

73

new ones are produced from the same place. This enables roots to occupy a small space as long as nutrients are in good supply — one of the features of their succes as container plants. It is also an indication of when palms should be transplanted or re-potted — early in the period of maximum growth.

Leaves — are evergreen and each lives for several years; the number of leaves on a mature plant remains fairly constant — as a leaf drops, a new one appears from within the crown, and thus the palm gains height. Scars on palm trunks are the marks of the leaf bases where they have clasped the trunk. The first leaves produced from a seed are grass-like; mature leaves can be palmate (fan), with a broad spreading blade that may divide into radiating arms, or pinnate (feather), a compound leaf with a central stalk and many side leaflets. The latter has a variation, bipinnate or fish-tail.

Temperature — most indoor conditions suit palms from warm temperate and sub-tropical regions. Though higher temperatures are preferred by most palms, they adapt well where the daily variation is between 13°C (55°F) and 25°C (77°F), though little growth will occur if the temperature remains below 16°C (61°F) for long periods. While needing good ventilation, palms must be protected from draughts and sudden changes in temperature.

Humidity — the ideal is around 60%; low humidity (20-30%) for too long results in lacklustre foliage with tips beginning to turn brown. Increase humidity by sponging and/or misting foliage, especially in warm weather, by grouping several plants together, or by double potting. If porous pots are used, the space is filled with moss or bark kept damp.

Light — most palms prefer bright, indirect light for growth, but tolerate low light levels. When there is a single light source, pots must be rotated regularly so plants do not develop unevenly.

Water — an actively growing palm will need copious amounts of water; in hot, dry rooms plants need more frequent waterings to replace that lost through transpiration. In winter and in cool rooms, less moisture is required. Perfect drainage is necessary; they do not tolerate wet feet.

Feeding: — use half strength liquid feeds every four to six weeks when actively growing.

Propagation — from seed or "off-shoots" of multi-stemmed species.

Hints — several different-sized palms of the same species in a single pot give a fuller effect. It is a wise practice to spell palms outdoors in

spring or summer in a warm, shaded place to freshen foliage and to promote new growth. Never put potted palms from inside into full sun; the foliage will burn. Use extra crushed pumice in the potting mix to ensure efficient drainage. Mealy bug and scale insects are the pests to watch for.

Varieties — *Chamaedorea* ("Parlour Palm"); *Chamaedorea seifritzii* (has multiple trunks); *Chamaedorea erumpens* ("Bamboo Palm"); *Linospadix monostachya* ("Walking Stick Palm"); *Howea forsteriana* and *H.belmoreana* ("Kentia" or "Thatch Palm"); *Phoenix roebelenii* (miniature Date Palm); *Rhapis humilis* ("Lady Palm").

Page 68 – *Chamaedorea elegans, the 'Parlour Palm', has had a name change to Collinia elegans - either name may be seen on plant labels. This small, very elegant palm is native to the rainforest areas of Mexico so it grows naturally in shade. It has gained great popularity as an indoor plant because of its ability to adjust to a range of light conditions. It likes a warm, humid atmosphere so needs to be misted regularly to maintain good looks. It is seldom more than 1.5m indoors.*

Page 69 – *Howea is the current botanical name of the ever-popular 'Kentia' palm. There are two species, both native to Lord Howe Island. They are considered the most suitable of all palms for use as indoor plants. They will tolerate low light areas but prefer bright, indirect light. 2.15 to 2.45m high indoors can be expected.*

Page 70 – *Phoenix roebelenii is commonly called dwarf, pygmy or miniature date palm. The fronds have a pendant growth habit and are tougher than their dainty appearance suggests. They like bright, indirect light to grow well - will slowly reach 120cm indoors.*

Pelargonium

Family *Geraniaceae*, a genus of 250 species with wide distribution — by far the greatest numbers coming from Africa. These are probably the best-known and most widely grown of all summer flowering container plants. Modern pelargoniums are mostly of hybrid origin, with a comprehensive colour range and attractive foliage. They make excellent container plants indoors or out. The dwarf and miniature forms are very suitable for indoors. *Geranium* is a separate genus of the same family.

Temperature — not hardy; enjoy summer heat.

Humidity — not a critical factor.

Light — bright light; enjoy full sun.

Water — allow pots to dry out between waterings in growing season, then water thoroughly; need very little water in winter.

Feeding — not necessary if re-potted annually. Diluted liquid feeds can be used sparingly — too much and they produce foliage at the expense of flowers.

Hints — re-pot regularly; they do not like to be pot-bound. Drainage is very important; add extra drainage material to mix. Prune back after flowering. Maintain a steady supply of new plants from cuttings; many are best renewed annually. Many of the "Zonals" have foliage that provides excellent winter colour.

Propagation — from cuttings taken in summer and autumn.

Varieties — *P. x domesticum* ("Regal Pelargonium"), has deep-veined leaves with toothed edges; flowers on short stems are large and showy with a contrasting blotch at the base of the petals; can be double or frilled; large, medium or small bushes are long-lived. *P. x hortorum* ("Zonal Pelargonium"), derived from *P.zonale* and *P.inquinans*, has smaller plants than the regals, also smaller flowers in compact heads on longer stems; rounded leaves have brown or mauve markings — some grown entirely for beautiful foliage. *P.peltatum* ("Ivy-leaved Pelargonium") are sprawling plants with shiny succulent leaves, single or double flowers on tall stems — excellent for hanging baskets.

Peperomia

Family *Piperaceae*, over 500 species in this genus of annual or perennial, evergreen, low-growing plants. Most come from the tropical rain forests of Central and South America, where they grow either terrestrially or as epiphytes. Selected as indoor plants because of their beautifully marked and shaped foliage. They produce curious long stemmed spikes of small white flowers.

Temperature — steady warmth, with a minimum of 10°C (50°F).

Humidity — high.

Light — bright, indirect.

Water — keep evenly damp in summer, much drier in winter.

Feeding — half strength every two months.

Propagation — stem or leaf cuttings.

Hints — used alone, in mixed planters, ideal in a dish garden or terrarium. The fleshy leaves of these plants allow them to adapt well to indoor conditions. They tolerate dry atmosphere and occasional neglect better than many other plants. Best watered from below. Re-pot annually.

Varieties — many species and cultivars are on offer: *P. sandersii* ("Watermelon Peperomia") has oval leaves patterned in silver and blue/green, exactly like a watermelon. *P. obtusifolia* "*variegata*" is a shrubby type with red and green stems and leaves cream marked with pale green. *P. caperata* ("Emerald Ripple") has pinkish stems with oval to heart-shaped leaves, dark green and deeply rippled. *P. scandens* "*variegata*" is a trailing type with grey/green and cream, heart-shaped leaves on pink stems.

Philodendron

Family *Araceae,* a genus of 200 species of evergreen climbing shrubs or small trees, native to tropical America with the family characteristics of aerial roots and arum-like flowers. Some species have entire heart-shaped leaves, while on others the foliage is deeply incised. The adaptability of these plants, the variety of leaf size and shape, and their long life expectancy, combine to make them highly successful indoor plants. These are tropical forest plants, and with a warm, moist atmosphere indoors they present no problems. They are divided into two groups — climbers which need sturdy support and the self-headers which need space. They look well in a large foyer, indoor courtyard, pool, sauna etc.

Temperature — average to warm, a minimum of 10°C (50°F).

Humidity — high; mist foliage in hot weather.

Light — diffused; never direct sun; tolerate low light.

Water — even moisture, never soggy; good drainage essential.

Feeding — every three or four months.

Propagation — stem cuttings.

Hints — do not use over-large pots or tubs; they benefit from a little crowding. For support, use a stout piece of tree fern or make a column of plastic netting filled with damp sphagnum moss; the aerial roots will weave through this. Keep leaves wiped free of dust.

Varieties — *P. andreanum* is a climber with large, velvety pendant olive-green leaves with a copper reverse. In pots, will be 2 metres high; there is a smaller juvenile form. *P. oxycardium* (syn. *P. scandens*), one of the most adaptable species, has glossy heart-shaped leaves; aerial roots on trailing stems will attach to anything. *P. erubescens* is a vigorous climber whose new leaves are rose-red; all foliage has maroon reverse; there are many named hybrids of this available: "Red Princess", "Redwings" or "Red Emerald", where all foliage has a reddish sheen and the young foliage and stems are quite red. *P. micans* ("Velvet Leaf Vine") is a very elegant small climber with small leaves tapering to a slender point; under sides have red coloration with silken sheen above. Now considered to be a juvenile form of *P. oxycardium.* This versatile genus is full of surprises — for instance, *P. gloriosum* has heart-shaped deep green leaves with a thin pink line round the margins, and cream veins.

Pilea

Family *Urticaceae*, a genus of 200 species of dwarf, evergreen annuals or perennials from all tropical countries, except Australia. These plants are attractive as indoor plants because of their variously coloured and textured foliage. Considered to be short-lived plants, but the insignificant nettle-like flowers produce seed readily so it is not difficult to have new plants ready as replacements. These small-scale plants look good enough to stand alone; also they suit plant arrangements where they can take advantage of extra humidity available.

Temperature — average to warm, minimum around 10°C (50°F).

Humidity — 50-70%.

Light — bright, indirect; not full sun.

Water — good drainage very important; be careful not to overwater; reduce watering in cold weather.

Feeding — every two months, in growing season.

Propagation — seed or cuttings.

Hints — mist plants in hot weather. Early in growing season pinch back tips to have compact plants. Have replacement plants growing-on; these are fast growing perennials and plants can become untidy or straggly in a couple of years.

Varieties — species include: *P. cadierei* ("Aluminium Plant"), with blue/green leaves with raised silver splashes between veins. *P. microphylla* (syn. *muscosa*), called "Artillery Plant" because when ripe the pollen is visibly discharged from the flowers; it forms a mat of fern-like foliage. *P. nummulariaefolia* also has tiny leaves and a spreading habit — considered a fine ground cover for terrarium. *P. pubescens* (syn. *P. involucrata*) has deeply quilted brownish-green leaves set in pairs, each pair set crosswise to the pair below. There are many other forms.

Portulacaria (Jade Plant)

This is a monotypic genus of the family *Portulaceae*. It is native to South Africa where, in times of drought, its succulent leaves and stems provide wholesome fodder for all classes of herbivorous animals. In containers, the plants are valued for adaptability to a wide range of rigorous growing conditions. They are much daintier than the species of *Crassula* which also carry the common name of "Jade Plant". They have an interesting angular growth that is easy to train; they are effective as bonsai.

Temperature — tolerate everything but frost.

Humidity — not important.

Light — do best in bright light, but tolerate low light conditions.

Water — need the minimum of moisture, but drainage must be very free.

Feeding — annual re-potting seems all that is necessary.

Propagation — cuttings of young shoots allowed to dry for two days before insertion into sand.

Hints — can be 2 metres high but are not difficult to keep trimmed to any size; do best in wide containers with extra drainage material added to mix.

Varieties — *P. afra* is the species. There is an attractive red-stemmed form with dark green leaves. A variegated form has leaves of a paler green edged with cream; it is not as robust as the species. All make ideal specimen plants in an environment subject to extremes.

Primula

Family *Primulaceae*, a genus of over 500 species widely distributed through the temperate regions of the Northern Hemisphere, especially in China and the Himalayas. It is a genus of woodland plants growing naturally in moist valleys beside streams in semi-shade. The primrose, cowslip, polyanthus, auricula all belong to this genus. In a temperate climate they are valued open garden plants. In recent years many species have become popular as winter flowering pot plants for use indoors.

Temperature — these are cool climate plants so heated rooms are not suitable; they like it cool to average — 10-16°C (50-61°F).

Humidity — 50-70%.

Light — partial shade, indirect sunlight.

Water — even, moist conditions, good drainage; must not dry out.

Feeding — need good nutrition through growing/flowering season.

Propagation — all can be grown from seed; perennials can be increased by division after flowering.

Hints — indoors, keep pots turned regularly to maintain straight stems. Remember, these are cool climate plants; too much warmth results in poorly growing plant and shortened flowering season. Check if plants are root-bound and re-pot when necessary; these plants must not be short of water when flowering and pots are difficult to moisten when roots have filled available space. Keep dead flowers removed.

Varieties — *P. malacoides* ("Fairy Primrose") is usually treated as an annual; it has lacy whorls of small flowers in white, pink, rose and lavender. *P. obconica* and *P. sinensis* are perennials though often treated as annuals; have larger flowers in shades of pink, white, lavender and purple on tall stems. *(P. obconica* has fine hairs to which some people are allergic.) *Primula x polyantha* (Polyanthus) hybrids in rainbow colours now available; can be purchased in flower, can be re-flowered. Easy to raise from seed each year.

Rhoeo (Moses-in-the-Bulrushes)

Family *Commelinaceae*, a monotypic genus native to Central America and related to the tradescantias and zebrinas, but differing from them by its upright, bushy habit of growth. It is grown indoors for its foliage, which is broad, dark green of colour, with rich purple undersides. It is used for contrast amongst the predominant greens of most indoor foliage plants. Insignificant white flowers are borne deep among boat-shaped bracts which appear from the leaf axils.

Temperature — do best with steady warmth, but tolerate a minimum of 10°C (50°F).

Humidity — high.

Light — suitable for low light areas.

Water — even moisture in summer; allow to become much drier in winter.

Feeding — half recommended strength in summer.

Propagation — from side shoots taken from base of plant.

Hints — good plant for a hanging basket; good contrast in plant groups.

Varieties — there is only one species, *R. spathacea*, sometimes listed as *R. discolor*. Other plants to seek to provide a similar colour contrast include from the same family, *Zebrina* and *Setcreasea purpurea* ("Purple Heart"), with foliage undersides that are deep purple; they need similar growing conditions to *Rhoeo* but more light to maintain good foliage colour. *Callisia elegans* ("Striped Inch Plant"), has dark green leaves, striped white, with purple reverse. *Setcreasea* and *Callisia* are propagated from jointed stems that break off easily.

Saintpaulia (African Violet)

From the family *Gesneriaceae* which provides many other fine indoor plants, this is a genus of six species from tropical East Africa. They are among the most popular of all indoor flowering plants. Virtues include size (compact enough for everyone to have room for at least one specimen), long flowering (usually autumn, winter, spring), attractive foliage (heart-shaped velvety leaves, sometimes variegated) and ease of propagation. Flowers are carried in stalked clusters, are similar in shape to a broad-petalled violet, 2-3cm across, in an amazing range of shades of pink, blue, magenta, purple, as well as white.

Temperature — need steady warmth, with a minimum of 16°C (61°F).

Humidity — constant, at least 50%.

Light — maximum, bright, indirect, though a little early morning sun is beneficial.

Water — even; allow surface of mix to become just dry between waterings, then water thoroughly from top or bottom; do not splash foliage unless it can be dried quickly.

Feeding — soluble plant food every two or three weeks after flowering.

Propagation — seed, leaf cuttings or division.

Hints — a stable environment in a draught-free situation is most important. Light is considered the critical factor in flowering and growing African Violets well — too strong, and they produce tight, stocky foliage; too poor, and new growth will be spindly, weak and no flowers will be produced. If humidity is too low, buds may drop off and foliage, instead of being flat, will curve down.

Varieties — *S.ionantha* and its thousands of cultivars, now far removed from the species. Hybridising has produced many new forms in flowers and foliage. The only satisfactory way is to purchase flowering plants.

Scindapsus

Family *Araceae*, a genus of 20 species of climbing herbaceous plants, usually rooting from the stem, native to tropical Asia and the Pacific. Those in cultivation are grown for attractive foliage. They have short aerial roots and need the support of a piece of tree-fern or a column made from nylon mesh filled with sphagnum moss.

Temperature — average to warm.

Humidity — high.

Light — bright, indirect.

Water — plenty of water in growing season; reduce quantity in cold weather. Mix can become slightly dry between waterings.

Feeding — each fortnight when growing.

Propagation — division or stem cuttings.

Hints — coloured leaf types need bright light to maintain colour, but not direct sun, which will scorch leaves. If old plants become leggy or too large for space, they can be pruned back in spring; use the prunings to propagate new plants.

Varieties — much name changing has been the lot of one species. It began as *Pothos,* became *Scindapsus,* and is now *Rhaphidophora.* I have left it with its second name as it is still seen labelled so in plant shops. *S. aureus* is native to the Solomon Islands. It is a large, vigorous, fleshy vine with pointed oval leaves that increase in size as they mature and the further they climb; they are dark green with yellow markings. There is a variety, "Marble Queen", on which the variegation is white. It is not as strong a grower as aureus, which needs a very stout tall pole to climb or can be allowed to hang. Where there is a shortage of room it can be replaced regularly with young plants. *S. pictus* ("Silver Vine" or Satin Pothos) is a very different plant, much smaller, with heart-shaped matt leaves marked pale green on dark. The variety "argyraeus" has leaves marked silver on dark green.

Sinningia (Gloxinia)

Family *Gesneriaceae*, a genus of 20 species of usually low-growing, hairy, herbaceous plants native to Brazil. The summer flowering pot plants called Gloxinias have been developed from crosses of species and selections of variations in the progeny of *S. speciosa*. These plants grow from a tuber and are among the most exciting flowering pot plants of summer with large, velvety, trumpet-shaped blooms in a range of rich stained-glass colours of red, blue and purple. Given favourable conditions, they remain in full bloom for many weeks.

Temperature — average warmth.

Humidity — high, with good ventilation.

Light — bright, indirect.

Water — keep mix evenly moist, do not over-water, and avoid splashing water on foliage.

Feeding — every seven to 10 days.

Propagation — seed or from pieces of tuber with a growing eye.

Hints — after flowering, reduce watering as leaves begin to fade. Gloxinias are usually dormant for about three months. Start tubers into growth in spring; when they are sprouting well, re-pot into fresh mix, water lightly until leaf growth is established, then resume regular care. It is generally advised to pinch out all but three of the strongest shoots to develop a sturdy plant.

Varieties — most gardeners begin a collection of Gloxinias with a plant in flower; they are usually on the market in late spring/early summer.

Spathiphyllum

A genus of about 30 species of almost stemless perennials — most from tropical America, some from Malaya. They belong to the family *Araceae*, so their relatives include *Aglaonema, Dieffenbachia, Caladium* and *Anthurium,* for which they are often mistaken, though their foliage is thinner and the bract is always white, and they are much hardier. Being evergreen, they are all-season ornamentals; the leaves are spear-shaped, shiny green, and rise in a cluster from the base of the plant. Flowers consist of a large white spathe with a cream spadix carried on long stems above the foliage; they appear at any time throughout the year and can last several months on the plant.

Temperature — preferably average to warm, but tolerate a minimum of 10°C (50°F).

Humidity — high; too dry and leaves brown at the edges.

Light — do well in low light areas; full sun not suitable.

Water — be liberal with water in hot weather, reduce water supply in low temperatures; should not dry out.

Feeding — every two months.

Propagation — by division any time the plant is not in flower.

Hints — mist foliage in hot weather to maintain humidity; sponge leaves to keep a fresh look. Re-pot in spring; they do best in pots a little on the small side. In dry atmosphere they can be troubled with red spider mite. Do well in an enclosed spa pool area. These plants have a long life expectancy.

Varieties — *S. wallisii* ("White Sails") is considered a dwarf species — 20-30cm. *S. x "Mauna Log"* has a much larger, fragrant flower, but is considered less robust. *S. x "Clevelandii"* ("Peace Lily") can be 90cm. Other species are *S. cannifolium* and *S. cochlearispathum.*

Succulents

1. *Sansevieria* — "Mother-in-Law's Tongue"

Family *Liliaceae*, a genus of 50 species of evergreen perennial plants growing from thick, short rhizomes, native to southern and tropical Africa, where the fibres of *S.trifasciata* are a source of hemp. They are grown outdoors in frost-free climates (often seen as small hedges in the islands of the Pacific), but elsewhere are prized as indoor plants for their decorative leaves, fragrant flowers and high survival rate against most odds.

Temperature — their preference is for constant warmth, but tolerate a wide range of temperatures, with a minimum of 10°C (50°F).

Humidity — look their best when humidity is high, but adapt to dry atmosphere.

Light — bright, indirect, but tolerate low light areas.

Water — should be soaked thoroughly, then allowed to dry out before the next soaking. As with other succulent plants, Sansevieria leaves have a tendency to rot at the base if over-watered, especially in winter. Perfect drainage is essential.

Feeding — monthly through spring and summer only.

Propagation — from suckers, division of crowded plants or from leaf cuttings of all-green species. Leaves are cut horizontally into sections about 5cm long; allow to dry out a little before inserting into damp sand in a warm place.

Hints — keep leaves free from dust; mist when atmosphere is very dry, Sansevieria will flower in late spring when conditions have been warm enough during the previous year.

Varieties — *S.trifasciata* is the species with leaves 60-80cm high and 5cm wide, broadly banded with silver-grey markings. The cv "Laurentii" — has broad yellow margins to leaves. *S.hahnii* — low growing, with short, broad leaves in rosette form, dark green, marked gold. "Golden Hahnii" — almost completely gold, with darker markings.

2. Kalanchoe

Family *Crassulaceae*, a genus of 100 species now including *Bryophyllum*, all succulent sub-shrubs from tropical and southern Africa, the eastern Mediterranean, India and China. They are very popular garden and house plants because they adapt well to differing environments, are quick to increase, have great variety of foliage form and most of them flower in winter. Some flowers are drooping bells in subdued colours; others have very bright colours and are held erect in clusters.

Temperature — not fussy, though a minimum of 10°C (50°F) is recommended; will tolerate to 5°C (40°F) for short periods.

Humidity — low to average.

Light — full sun or bright, indirect.

Water — need good moisture supply through spring/summer growing season; drainage must be excellent; reduce water in autumn/winter.

Feeding — every two to four weeks after flowering and through growing season.

Propagation — seed, leaf or stem cuttings. Some species, such as *K.tubiflora* (syn.*Bryophyllum*), form complete plantlets along edges of leaves — these are removed and potted on. Cuttings should be allowed to dry out for a day or so before being inserted into damp sand.

Hints — terrestrial succulents such as these require extra drainage material, coarse sand or crushed pumice, in potting mix to ensure perfect drainage. After flowering, remove faded stalks, and water only when mix is becoming dry; when new growth begins, increase water applications and begin to fertilise. These are "short day" plants, so flowering can be manipulated.

Varieties — *K.blossfeldiana* has shiny green leaves sometimes edged with red, showy heads of scarlet flowers; there are selected forms with yellow and pink flowers and a dwarf variety "Tom Thumb". *K.pumila* — a compact plant with silvery leaves and pink flowers. *K.tomentosa* ("Panda Plant") — leaves covered in silver hairs that become rust at the serrated tip.

3. Lithops — "Living Stones"

Family *Aizoaceae*, the same family as *Mesembryanthemum, Lamparanthus* and *Conophytum*, a genus of 70 species of curious, succulent plants from South Africa, where they grow in desert conditions in sand and gravel with little soil. These small (maximum height around 2.5cm), endearing plants are all miracles of camouflage. Each growth consists of two fleshy leaves united except for a fissure across the top through which the flowers emerge. The growths are solitary or in small clumps, conical, oval or rounded to conserve the greatest possible volume of water. The upper surface has markings and/or colourings in greys, fawns, browns and greens so they closely resemble the pebbles among which they grow, and thus are camouflaged from browsing animals. The daisy-like flowers, which can be bigger than the plant, are stemless, white or yellow, and appear from late summer to mid-autumn. These are wondrous plants, suitable for shallow trays in a warm, sunny position indoors.

Temperature — not hardy, they like steady warmth through the year; aim at a minimum of 16°C (61°F).

Humidity — not a factor, but require good ventilation.

Light — bright all year; some full sun each day through the growing/flowering season.

Water — in growing season only, and then sparingly; allow mix to dry out between waterings.

Feeding — should not be necessary.

Propagation — from seed.

Hints — use a coarse, gravelly mix, top with a layer of pebbles, add a few larger stones to match the colours of the plants. Re-pot every two or three years. Usually available from specialist nurseries.

Variations — species to look for: *L.salicola, L.bella, L.optica, L.turbiniformis.*

Thunbergia (Clock Vine)

Acanthaceae is the family most often listed for *Thunbergia*, which makes them relatives of other indoor plants such as *Aphelandra* and *Fittonia,* though some authorities give them a family of their own. However, there are 200 species, mostly twining, annual or perennial plants from tropical Africa and South Africa and the warmer parts of Asia. These plants need warm, frost-free conditions, when they will flower freely. In cool climates, they are given glasshouse protection, grown as indoor plants or only the annuals grown. The vigorous species suit conservatories or garden rooms; the more modest species make excellent container plants for summer colour.

Temperature — steady warmth.

Humidity — average to high.

Light — full sun or bright, indirect light.

Water — keep mix evenly moist; good drainage is essential.

Feeding — every two weeks through growing/flowering season.

Propagation — seed, layers, cuttings.

Hints — all climbers will need some support; annuals can twine up a tripod of canes or trail or hang from planters, troughs or hanging baskets. When grown in full sun indoors, extra watering will be necessary. Watch for thrip damage.

Varieties — *T. alata*, ("Black-eyed Susan") has orange, tubular flowers opening to a flat disc, with several lobes centred with dark brown. It is a perennial, though usually treated as an annual as it grows readily from seed and produces masses of flowers from late spring to autumn. It has triangular leaves and thin stems, looks fragile but will grow three or four metres in a season. *T. gregorii (*syn. *T. gibsonii)* is similar, without the dark eye and has hairy foliage. Both are from Africa. From India come *T. grandiflora*, with sky blue flowers, and *T.mysorensis* with drooping sprays of reddish-brown and yellow flowers. Need plenty of room.

Zebrina

Family *Commelinaceae,* a genus of four species of evergreen pendulous plants from Mexico and southern United States. Closely related to and similar to *Tradescantia,* though not as hardy. They share the common name "Wandering Jew". These are ideal subjects for hanging baskets in a semi-shaded area.

Temperature — average, not hardy.

Humidity — high.

Light — bright, indirect; not full sun.

Water — even moisture.

Feeding — half recommended strength every two months.

Propagation — stem cuttings.

Hints — these plants are grown for their strongly-coloured foliage; it is well to remember that if they are over-fed the leaf colour may revert to mainly green. Once cuttings are struck and begin to grow, remove the growing tips to encourage branching. Once plants are passed their prime, it is best to replace them, several young plants to a single pot. This is the reason for making regular plantings of cuttings.

Varieties — *Z.pendula* has ovate leaves, purple beneath, green and purple above, with two silver bands. Its variety, "Quadricolor", has white and pink added to the colours of the species, and needs bright light to maintain colour. *Z.purpusii* is considered more vigorous and has leaves in various shades of purple. Though not considered among the choicest of indoor plants, members of the family *Commelinaceae* are easy to grow, fill a large space quickly, and provide strong colour.

Glossary

Aerial root — a root above soil level usually used for support, though moisture may be absorbed.

Areole — the swelling on a Cactus from which appear spines, hairs, flowers, etc.

Autotropic — able to build up food from simple inorganic compounds.

Axil — the upper angle between the stem and the leaf growing from it.

Cambium — a ring of dividing cells in a stem or root giving rise to secondary thickening.

Clavate — club-shaped.

Clones — all plants produced from one original parent plant (all cuttings, layers or runners), but not plants raised from seed of the plant.

Compound — (of leaves), having two or more leaflets.

Cultivar — a plant variety that has arisen in cultivation.

Dicotyledon (Dicot) — a flowering plant with two cotyledons (seed leaves) in each seed.

Diploid — having two sets of chromosomes per cell.

Epidermis — the outer layer of cells (the skin).

Epiphyte — a plant which grows on another but is not parasitic.

Genus — (used in plant classification), a group of closely related species.

Haploid — an organism having one set of chromosomes per cell, ie, half the normal number.

Hardy — capable of growing outside year-round without protection. A term used to describe a plant's tolerance of cold. A plant is half-hardy when it will resist moderate frosts.

Heel — a cutting removed with a "heel", or piece of the parent branch, attached to the base.

Herbaceous — a non-woody plant that dies back annually.

Hose-in-hose — a floral abnormality in which one perfect flower is carried in another, sometimes giving the appearance of having grown from the lower one.

Hybrid — a cross between two species.

Monocotyledon (Monocot) — a flowering plant with one cotyledon (seed leaf) in each seed.

Mucilaginous — like gum.

Node — a slightly swollen region on a stem where leaves and buds grow.

Palmate — shaped like an open hand.

Panicle — a branching cluster of flowers.

Photosynthesis — the process by which green plants use the energy of light to make glucose from carbon dioxide and water.

Pseudobulb — a thickened, modified, above-ground stem found in some orchids; it serves to store nutrients.

Raceme — a stem with flowers along its length.

Saprophytic — (for instance, fungi), a plant which lives on decayed matter; as a result it contains no chlorophyll and is unable to manufacture food with the aid of sunlight.

Spadix — an elongated raceme of sessile flowers surrounded by a spathe, the stem of the flower spike usually long and fleshy.

Spathe — a bract or leaf-like structure protecting a spadix, sometimes coloured and flower-like.

Species — a group of plants all possessing the same constant, distinctive characteristics.

Spike — an inflorescence with sessile flowers on an elongated, unbranched axis.

Stomata — the "breathing pores" of a plant, microscopic openings which carry out gaseous interchange between plant and atmosphere.

Tender — denotes a low tolerance to cold conditions.

Terminal — shoot at the end of a stem.

Terrestrial — plants that grow on the earth's surface, as opposed to epiphytes.

Umbel — group of flowers growing from a common point.

Xerophytic — a plant adapted to living in arid conditions.

Index